MARY•ANNE•BAUER SIMPLY ENTERTAINING

To Nancy —
Who is ever
"entertaining!"

SECOND EDITION

MaryAnneBauer

Table of Contents

Introduction

To me, successful entertaining is a celebration of the senses: Food that intrigues the taste buds. Presentation and decoration which catch the eye. Good conversation and laughter to lift the spirit.

And I'm delighted to tell you that this can be achieved even if you *are* a busy person!

For years, I've shared my easy, inexpensive, yet very special entertaining ideas with viewers of AM Northwest. Here, I'm sharing them with you. In addition to creative recipes that are quick and do-ahead, you'll also find many other tips to help you enjoy more time with your guests, while you spend less time in the kitchen.

All this comes to you with my very best wishes. May all your future celebrations be SIMPLY ENTERTAINING!

Mary Anne Bauer

The Party Planner

The secret to successful entertaining is planning. Whether you've invited two or twenty, following these few basic guidelines will make entertaining a joy.

- **Remind yourself why you are entertaining.** To celebrate a special occasion? To return a favor? For business? Or just to get friends together? Whatever the reason, entertaining is a gift of yourself and you want it to be special. Let this be your inspiration!

- **Determine what kind of entertaining it will be.** Your time, energy and budget will help you decide if it will be formal or informal; sit-down or buffet; cocktail party, dinner, brunch, open house, a simple dessert or even a potluck.

- **Begin planning.** No matter what kind of party you are giving, following these simple steps will keep you calm, out of the kitchen and enjoying your own party.

- **Make a guest list.** Keep in mind how many people you can accommodate comfortably for the type of entertaining. Try to include a good mix of guests appropriate for the type of party planned.

- **Set a date and time.**

- **Plan invitations.** Decide whether they will be extended by phone, written note or printed invitation and set a date by which this should be accomplished. Keep a checklist of responses.

- **Plan a menu.** Again consider the available time and budget. Include a contrast in flavors, colors, textures, temperatures and shapes of food and the courses. It is important that the majority of dishes be prepared in advance. Too many items needing a great deal of last minute attention result in a hassled host or hostess.

- **Make a list of everything that must be done.** Separate it into the following categories:

  Groceries – Review each recipe for items to be purchased. Don't forget garnish. Check the list again the day of the party, in case something you thought you had was accidentally used.

  Special party needs – These include cocktail napkins, candles, ice, flowers and other such items you'll need to purchase.

  Make a time table for when you'll clean house, polish silver, set table, arrange the centerpiece, check the linens and so on.

  Food preparation schedule – List the items which can be done ahead and those which need last day attention. If there are too many last day items, go back and revise the menu.

  Serving pieces. Using the menu as a guide, decide on trays, bowls and platters which should be gathered at the ready.

  Items to be borrowed – Will you need a punch bowl, extra large coffee pot, extra glasses?

  Write up a party-day time line and post it. List the entire menu noting cooking times and temperatures, when items should be taken out of the refrigerator, when and what items need garnishing. Also schedule when you should pour the water, light the candles, heat the rolls and make the coffee.

- **Set the table** the night before the party.
- **Walk through the party.** Just think of it as a dress rehearsal. Reviewing details ahead of time will help make the party run smoothly.

  Check the front door. Is it fresh and clean to greet guests?

  Is there a place for coats and are there plenty of hangers?

4

Is there enough seating? What about ashtrays and coasters?

For a sit down affair, check each place setting for a missing fork or glass. For a buffet, check for convenient arrangement of utensils, plates, food items and so on.

Is the preparation area in order? Is it safe and easy to plug in appliances? Is there a place for dishes coming out of the oven?

Is serving and clearing well planned: How will you handle the dirty dishes? And did you reserve an area for serving dessert?

Check the bathroom for guest towels, soap and tissues.

- At least a week in advance, **select a comfortable outfit** that you particularly like. Check that it is clean and pressed, select accessories. Put all items together to avoid any last minute searching.

- **Plan plenty of time to get dressed** and review last minute details. You'll want to take a leisurely bath so you'll be refreshed when guests arrive. (If you're throwing yourself together as the doorbell rings, you'll be hassled before you begin.)

- **Allow extra time for each task.** Sometimes things take longer than planned.

- **Relax.** It's your party and you should have a good time, too.

Creative Touches

SETTING THE SCENE

- **Greet your guests in a special way.** A grapevine or straw wreath on the front door is a friendly touch. Change it with different ribbons and trims for each season (a nesting bird for spring; silk or real flowers for summer; small flags and red, white and blue ribbons for the 4th of July; dried flowers for fall; ornaments for Christmas. You get the idea!)

- **Warm up the room.** A cozy winter fire is a nice welcome for guests. Remember to have enough wood ready for burning throughout the party. Try replacing several white light bulbs with pink ones to add a rosy glow to any room.

- **Spice up the house.** Simmer several cinnamon sticks and some whole cloves in a small pan of water. It will fill the house with a delightful homey scent.

- **Soothe the ears.** Quiet background music can help the mood of a party. Just be sure it doesn't interfere with conversation.

CANDLE MAGIC

Candles add a cozy and festive glow to any gathering. Use them liberally to create a special party mood, keeping safety in mind at all times. Greens used with candles should be very fresh. Never leave burning candles unattended. Avoid placing candles close to curtains or where they might be knocked over.

When you use candles at the dinng table, make certain they're above or below eye level of guests.

- **Group candles.** For a dramatic look, use candles in the same color, but of different sizes and shapes.

- **Mix and match.** You also can add interest to a candle collection by gathering a variety of compatible holders together.

- **Add greens and flowers.** Arrange candles in votive holders, and encircle with fresh greenery. Or try placing three large column candles of different sizes on a small tray or mirror, surrounded with flowers or several sprigs of greenery.
- **Yet another idea:** place a large column candle in a clear glass bowl, then float flowers and leaves in water around it.
- **Use fruits and vegetables.** They can be charming candle holders! Use an apple corer to cut out the center of an apple, leaving ½" at the bottom. Place a candle in the center hole. Artichokes make attractive holders. Simply remove some of the center leaves, then push a candle into the middle.

CANDLE TIPS
- **Place candles in the freezer.** If you do so for several hours before using, it will make them burn more slowly.
- **Burning candles help to remove cigarette smoke** from the air. This can be especially important if you invite guests who smoke. Incidentally, a small bowl of vinegar placed out of the way, also will absorb smoke odors without any telltale vinegar smell.
- **Candle fitting.** Running hot water over the bottom of candles can help mold them to fit most holders.
- **Caution with scented candles.** Avoid using them in the same room as food. They interfere with the enjoyment of food aromas and taste.
- **Candles should not be lighted in the daytime.** Save them for evening gatherings. Be sure to have plenty of replacements.
- **A word on wicks.** When candles are new the wicks should be charred even though they will not be lighted for the occasion.

TABLE DECORATIONS
A centerpiece sets the mood for the table. Try some of these quick, easy and low cost ideas to turn a plain table into a

stunning background for your meal. Remember to keep center-pieces low enough for guests to easily see over them.

- **Gather up the greens.** Laurel, holly, ivy or a mixture of foliage can fill a bowl, a basket lined with a bowl or any attractive container. For color, tie a bow around the holder or make several double bows and tuck into greenery.

- **Highlight a special collection of objects**, ceramic figures, shells, tea cups, small vases, all can be used as a charming focal point for the table. Use them alone or with several small plants or flowers. Small items also can be placed at each individual place setting.

- **Use fresh fruits and vegetables.** They'll make a color-ful centerpiece any time of the year. Select perfectly shaped produce and arrange on a platter, or in a bowl or basket. (You have an instant centerpiece that can be eaten later.) Or use vegetables themselves as containers. Hollow out eggplant, pumpkins, or other vegetables in season, then fill with garden flowers or greens.

- **Decorate with beautiful loaves of bread.** On a small cutting board or in a napkin lined basket, arrange several loaves of uncut bread considering shape, texture and size. For example, use a long loaf of french bread with a small loaf of wheat and a round or braided loaf. Rolls in interesting shapes also can be added. Tuck straw flowers or a few shafts of wheat into the arrangement.

- **Make centerpieces seasonal.** In the fall arrange color-ful dried and pressed leaves with nuts and seasonal vegetables. Be sure to press leaves between pages of a weighted-down phone book before using. Or dip freshly gathered leaves into melted parafin to preserve them. For a spring arrangement, fill a basket with natural colored straw and add white or brown blown-out eggs.

- **Spring and summer flowers** are beautiful floating in a low clear glass bowl.

- When summer fruit is plentiful, **make an edible centerpiece** using watermelon draped with washed ivy leaves and vines which are attached with toothpicks. Cut a variety of melons and a pineapple into large chunks using a fluted cutter if desired. Spear each with a wooden skewer and push into the ivy covered watermelon.

- **For a winter centerpiece**, stud oranges with cloves and pile into a pyramid. Tuck laurel leaves in-between.

RIBBONS

- **Ribbons add a festive note of color** to the table. Tie a narrow ribbon to the stems of glasses, around a decanter or as a ring for each napkin. Let your imagination go! For example, at Christmas you could decorate clear glass cups with a ribbon and tie a little bell to each streamer.

- You also can use 2½"-3" wide ribbon to add color to the table itself. Run in rows down the length of the table on each side of the centerpiece.

- Try marking each place setting by running ribbons across the width of the table.

- For a buffet, roll napkin around flatware and tie with a ribbon. Stand in a basket for easy service.

BASKETS

- **Baskets** are a bargain decorating boon. We've mentioned using them for centerpieces, breads and rolls, buffet napkins and flatware. You also might try them as a holder for casserole dishes, nuts and snacks. With a little thought of your own, you'll undoubtedly find there is no end to their versatility!

PLACECARDS

- Use **placecards** for large sit-down dinners. It will alleviate the awkward problem of guests hovering about the table wondering where to sit. Write or print each guest's name on the front and back of the card, so it can be read from either side of the table. For newly acquainted guests, the cards also serve as a nice reminder of new names!

Napkin Folding

Something as simple as an attractively folded napkin can add pizzaz to an ordinary table. The fan shape is an elegant style and the candlestick, since it takes up only a couple of inches, is perfect for a crowded table. The lily offers a graceful, dramatic touch.

Fan-Tastic

1. Begin by folding napkins in half.
2. Make ¾" accordion pleats from the bottom, ⅔ of the way up the napkin.
3. Fold in half with accordion pleats on outside.
4. Fold right corner into rectangle. Piece should extend beyond fold beneath.
5. At this point napkin should look a little like a sailboat. Fold 1" piece under to form "stand."
6. Stand up and napkin will fan out.

Candlestick

1. Begin by making a triangle.
2. Form a 1½" hem at bottom of triangle.
3. Turn napkin over and place on side.
4. Roll, beginning at bottom point of napkin.
5. Leave 1" at end and tuck it into hem at bottom to secure fold.
6. Stand napkin up and it resembles a candle.

Lily

1. Begin by laying napkin on table and rolling tightly from one corner.
2. Bend and fold in half. Push into stemmed glass.
3. Turn down top edge of each end of roll to form two lilies.

Make-It-Yourself Parties

Make-It-Yourself Parties

Party goers feel right at home when they're in on the action. "Make-It-Yourself" parties are relaxed and comfortable for everyone — host or hostess and guest alike. With a minimum of do-ahead preparation, everyone can relax and enjoy the party. The guests do most of the work and they love it!

South of the Border Burgers

Hamburgers, juicy and hot from the grill, are unsurpassed on the list of All-American favorites. The fun comes at this summertime gathering when guests concoct their own open-faced burgers by adding any of a number of toppings. Team with chilled, 24-hour vegetable salad, hearty do-ahead beans and fast and fudgy brownies to create perfect summer-party fare. As a winter treat, broil burgers in oven.

MENU

Sangria
Layered Salad
South of the Border Burgers
Variety of Toppings
Taco Bread
Grilled Cheese Potatoes
Sweet and Sour Baked Beans
Triple-Fudge Brownies, page 96
Fresh Fruit

PARTY POINTERS

- A basket brimming with fresh fruit is a refreshing centerpiece and can be offered as a dessert.
- Try the watermelon centerpiece, page 5. If yours is a holiday party – Memorial Day, 4th of July or Labor Day – include some flags in your table arrangement. Use 1" flags on picks to decorate salad and dessert.
- Use small plastic flower pots to hold hamburger toppings. toppings.
- Toast French bread slices on grill or in oven and place under hamburger to catch juices.

Sangria

A fruity flavor of Mexico.

1   750 ml bottle red wine
½   cup sugar
    juice of 4 medium lemons
    juice of 1 large orange
1   medium lemon, sliced
1   medium orange, sliced

In a large pitcher, combine wine, sugar, juices. Stir well. Add sliced lemon and orange. Serve over crushed ice in chilled glasses. Six servings. Double or triple recipe for larger groups.

Layered Salad

It's hard to believe how crisp all the ingredients stay in this do ahead salad.

1   medium head lettuce, shredded
1   cup celery, chopped
1   cup water chestnuts, sliced
1   green pepper, chopped
1   bunch green onions, chopped
1   10-ounce package frozen petite peas, uncooked
1   cup Best Foods mayonnaise
½   cup sour cream
¼   cup Parmesan cheese
2   eggs, hard-cooked, then grated
½   pound bacon cooked, drained and crumbled or
     ½   cup bacon bits
2-3 medium tomatoes, cut in wedges

In a large clear glass bowl layer lettuce, celery, water chestnuts, green pepper, green onions, peas. Mix mayonnaise with sour cream and spread over entire top of salad, sealing all the way to the edges. Sprinkle with Parmesan cheese, grated egg, and bacon. Cover with plastic wrap and refrigerate overnight. Garnish with a pinwheel of tomato wedges and serve. Serves 10-12.

Variations:
- Use ½ cup grated Cheddar cheese in place of Parmesan.
- Use torn spinach in place of half of lettuce.
- Add a layer of chopped or sliced black or green olives.

Taco Bread

1½   cups butter, softened
1   tablespoon dry taco seasoning mix
1   loaf French bread

In a small bowl mix butter and taco seasoning mix. Spread on each slice of bread. Toast bread on grill.

South of the Border Burger

No two burgers will be alike. Each of these knife and fork burgers will reflect its guest creator.

3 pounds lean ground beef (3-4 burgers per pound)

Grill burgers on barbeque to desired degree of doneness. Place each on slice of grilled taco bread.

Toppings for South of the Border Burgers

1 cup guacamole
2 cups shredded lettuce
1 cup chopped onion
2 cups tomatoes, chopped
2 cups Cheddar and/or jack cheese, shredded
½ pint sour cream
1 pound bacon, cooked and crumbled
1 16-ounce can black olives, sliced
1 12-ounce bottle salsa
1 15-ounce can chiles, chopped

Guests place cooked hamburgers on buttered, toasted bread. Then they choose any or all of the toppings to create their own perfect burger. Serves 8-10.

Grilled Cheese Potatoes

Fluffy baked potatoes with melting cheese.

8 potatoes
     cooking oil
1½ cups Cheddar cheese, shredded
1½ cups sour cream
8 green onions, chopped

Brush each potato with oil and wrap in foil. Grill over medium coals about 1 hour. Turn over and bake another 45 minutes to 1 hour. Open foil; slit potato and top with mixture of shredded cheese, sour cream and green onion. Allow cheese to melt and serve. Serves 8.

Sweet and Sour Baked Beans

Hearty and satisfying.

1 pound hamburger
½ pound bacon, cut into pieces
3 large onions
2 cloves garlic, crushed
1 15-ounce can kidney beans, drained
1 15-ounce can butter beans, drained
1 32-ounce can pork and beans with sauce
1 teaspoon liquid smoke (optional)
1 teaspoon dry mustard or 1 tablespoon
  prepared mustard
½ cup vinegar
⅔ cup brown sugar
¼ cup tomato sauce or catsup

In large frying pan, brown hamburger and saute bacon, onion and garlic. Drain well. Add kidney beans, butter beans, lima beans and pork and beans. Mix mustard, vinegar, brown sugar and tomato sauce and add. Pour into baking dish. Bake 1 hour at 350 degrees.

Variations:

- Serve Sweet and Sour Baked Beans over buttered and toasted hamburger or hot dog buns. Or serve over hot dogs in buns.
- Use 1-2 pounds of sausage in place of hamburger and bacon in bean recipe.

Triple-Fudge Brownies, page 96.

Coffee Party

The exotic aroma of coffee greets guests at this easy afternoon party – perfect on a cold winter day, or use the idea for an after-theatre get-together. Guests sample several coffees, adding liqueurs, whipped cream or chocolate. Some crisp cookies and candy add the perfect sweet touch. Chocolate cups filled with whipped cream or liqueur float in coffee until melted, adding a truly elegant touch.

MENU
2 Coffees
1 Decaffeinated Coffee
Whipped Cream
Liqueurs
Chocolate Shot
Crisp Cookies
Chocolate Truffles
Quick Nut Clusters

NOTE: Any of the crisp cookies on page 125-126 would be a nice accompaniment for coffee.

PARTY POINTERS

- A trip to your favorite coffee shop will give you some ideas on types of coffee to serve. Be sure to offer one decaffeinated coffee for those guests who prefer it.

- Arrange several pots of coffee on a buffet table; make a

small signs out of folded plain index cards with the names of the coffees. Place near pots.

- Offer sugar, perhaps raw sugar too, a glass bowl of whipped cream and a bowl of chocolate shot. Provide a bowl of cinnamon sticks to use as flavorful stirrers.
- Of course, a variety of crisp cookies and some chocolate candy are just the right accompaniment.
- A tray with several liqueurs is nice to offer.
- See Liqueurs you make yourself on page 173-175.

Chocolate Truffles

These ultra-rich creamy candies are perfect to savor with a cup of coffee.

- 1 8-ounce package unsweetened chocolate
- 1 4-ounce package sweet cooking chocolate
- 1 14-ounce can sweetened condensed milk
   chopped nuts or flaked coconut

Melt chocolates together over hot water or on low power in a microwave oven. Add condensed milk and mix until smooth. Cool a few minutes and then shape into balls, using 1 teaspoon per ball. Roll in nuts or coconut. Freeze or store in covered container. To serve, place each ball in a tiny candy paper cup and arrange on a pretty doily covered tray. Makes 3-4 dozen.

Quick Nut Clusters

Make these in minutes. Try melting the chocolates in a dish in the microwave for about 1½ minutes.

1 6-ounce package semi-sweet chocolate chips
1 6-ounce package sweet chocolate chips
2 cups salted peanuts or slivered almonds

Melt chocolate in double boiler over hot (not boiling) water. Stir in peanuts until well coated. (For sweeter cluster, shake peanuts in strainer first to remove excess salt.) Spoon teaspoonful onto foil. Chill until firm. Makes 1½ pounds.

Chocolate Cups, page 62-63.

Sweetened Condensed Milk

1 cup plus 2 tablespoons nonfat dry milk crystals
½ cup warm water
¾ cup white sugar

Blend all ingredients in blender or food processor about three minutes. Refrigerate. Use in recipes calling for sweetened condensed milk.

Sweetened Condensed Milk #2

1½ cups sugar
⅔ cups hot water
¼-½ cup butter or margarine
2 cups nonfat dry milk crystals

Heat sugar, water and butter or margarine in a saucepan or in glass container in microwave. Simmer gently several minutes, stirring. Pour into a large-capacity food processor or blender (or prepare half batch at a time). Blend in dry milk. Process or blend about three minutes. Refrigerate. Use in recipes calling for sweetened condensed milk.

Donut and Cider Party

A cool, crisp evening and a house full of good friends gathered 'round a crackling fire set the scene for this super-simple party. Puffy, hot donuts fried by the guests are rolled in a choice of frostings, sugars, nuts and other toppings. Serve apple cider in a punch bowl made from a hollowed-out pumpkin — the perfect fall touch.

MENU
Cold Cider
Hot Mulled Cider
Frozen-Dough Donuts
Vanilla Frosting Glaze
Chocolate Frosting Glaze
Various Donut Coatings

PARTY POINTERS
- Arrange to have two electric frying pans so guests don't have to wait to fry their donuts.
- Be sure to keep all children away from the donut frying area.
- Serve the hot cider from a crock pot to keep it warm throughout the evening.
- Offer coffee for those guests who prefer it to a sweet drink.
- Plan on about 3 donuts per guest.

Hot Mulled Cider

2 quarts apple cider
½ cups brown sugar, packed
1 teaspoon whole cloves
1 teaspoon whole allspice
3 sticks of cinnamon
1 fresh lemon, sliced with peel

In a large pan heat cider with sugar, until the sugar is dissolved. Add cloves, allspice, cinnamon sticks and lemon slices. Simmer 10 minutes. Remove spices and serve. Makes 16, 8-ounce servings.

Also offer cold cider for those guests who prefer a cold drink. In this case, chill the cider well and simply serve from a large chilled pitcher.

Frozen-Dough Donuts

All you have to do to prepare this simple and delicious party food is thaw the bread dough for several hours — or overnight in refrigerator — and let your guests do the rest: cut, fry and coat donuts with any of the various toppings.

frozen bread dough (each loaf will make about
    12 donuts, 12 donut holes)
vegetable oil or shortening (enough to equal
    1½" in each electric frying pan)
pancake turner and tongs
donut cutters
paper towels

Allow dough to rest at room temperature for 45 minutes to an hour. Then have your guests roll the dough out to a thickness of ½" and cut their donuts. Let the dough rest another 15 minutes. Guests then place the donuts in an electric frying pan with 1½" oil heated to 375 degrees.

Donuts only take 2-3 minutes to cook. When they are light brown on the underside, turn them over and cook until puffed and golden.

Remove with a pancake turner and place on several thicknesses of paper towels to drain. While still warm, have guests roll their donuts in sugars, or frost and dip into their favorite toppings.

Donut Coatings

This makes enough for 2 dozen donuts.

Vanilla Frosting Glaze

    ¼ cup milk
    1 teaspoon vanilla extract
    2 cups sifted confectioners' sugar

In medium bowl, blend milk and vanilla into sugar until smooth. Makes 2½ cups.

Chocolate Frosting Glaze

    4 squares unsweetened chocolate
    4 tablespoons butter or margarine
    ½ cup milk
    2 cups sifted confectioners' sugar
    2 teaspoons vanilla extract

In a double boiler or in microwave oven, melt chocolate and butter. In small saucepan heat milk. Mix chocolate with hot milk, sugar and vanilla until smooth. Makes 1½ cups.

Other Toppings

    Granulated sugar
    Cinnamon and sugar
    Powdered sugar
    Chocolate shot
    Coconut
    Walnuts, finely chopped
    Almonds, finely chopped

Fondue Party

The French word fondue means "to melt," and the technique of melting cheese or chocolate has been around for hundreds of years. For today's hostess this is an easy, relatively inexpensive, casual party. Make the entire evening a fondue party, or use the cheese fondue as an appetizer to a traditional dinner party. You could even make the dessert fondue a party in itself.

MENU
A Dry White Wine
Traditional Cheese Fondue
French Bread Cubes
Small Breadsticks
Vegetables
Chocolate Fondue
Cake Cubes, Cookies, Fruit

PARTY POINTERS
- An ideal way to seat guests is around a round dining room table or at a coffee table.
- If guests are seated at a long table, allow one fondue pot for every 4-6 people.
- Recipe for making your own condensed milk: page 19.
- Lightly steam broccoli, cauliflower and carrots if desired, for dipping.
- To accommodate a large group set up several small tables, each with its own pot of fondue.

- Have cheese grated and wine measured ahead of time.
- Keep in mind it takes 20-30 minutes to heat the wine and melt the cheese. With a large party you'll want a guest helper for each pot.
- Tell guests that the Swiss have a custom: anyone who loses his bread must pay with a kiss.
- For an instant dessert fondue, heat 1-2 jars Smucker's or Hershey's Hot Fudge Sauce.

Traditional Cheese Fondue

1   pound natural Swiss cheese, shredded
3   tablespoons flour
1-2 cloves garlic, cut in half
1½ cups dry white wine
1   tablespoon brandy or lemon juice,
    dash white pepper
    dash ground nutmeg
    French bread, cubed
    Breadsticks
    Fresh vegetables: cauliflower, broccoli,
      mushrooms, cherry tomatoes, carrots
    Fondue pot or chafing dish
    Long-handled fondue forks
    Small plate for each guest

In a medium-size bowl, toss shredded cheese with 3 tablespoons of flour until the cheese is well-coated. Rub the inside of the fondue pot with cut half of a garlic clove. Discard the garlic and pour wine into the fondue pot. Heat over low heat until small bubbles form on the bottom of the pan. Add brandy or lemon juice. Add cheese to hot wine a ½ cup at a time, stirring constantly until cheese is melted. Stir in pepper and nutmeg. Cut bread into 1″ cubes to use for dipping. To serve, keep fondue hot over table top burner. Provide long-handled fondue forks and small plate for each guest. Guests then dip speared bread into hot fondue, swirl, and eat all in one mouthful.

Large cubes of ham are also good for dipping.

24

Fantastic Fudge Fondue

Rich and velvety.

1 6-ounce package semi-sweet chocolate chips
2 tablespoons butter
1 can sweetened condensed milk, see page 19
2 tablespoons coffee flavored liqueur or
    1 tablespoon vanilla flavored extract
1 loaf pound cake
1 package crisp Pepperidge Farm cookies
   or Cookies, page 125-126
   fresh strawberries, sliced apples
   mandarin oranges, pineapple chunks

In a small heavy saucepan melt chocolate chips over medium heat. (Chocolate melts quickly and easily in a microwave oven. If you own one, try melting chocolate this way: place chocolate in glass container. Microwave for 30 seconds on low power. Add butter and microwave 30 seconds. Add sweetened condensed milk and microwave until mixture is hot.) If you're using conventional melting methods, continue in this fashion: stir in butter. Add sweetened condensed milk, liqueur or vanilla and salt. Cook, stirring constantly, until mixture is hot and thickened. Keep warm in fondue pot to serve. For dipping, provide pound cake cut into cubes, crisp cookies, fresh and canned fruit.

NOTE: Should mixture become too thick, simply add 1 tablespoon hot water until mixture is of desired consistency.

Omelette Party

Once a cook learns how to make an omelette, there's no end to its variations. For this party each omelette is made to order with fillings selected by the guests. It's a casual entertaining idea that uses the kitchen as part of the entertaining center. You could even let your guests cook their own omelettes or have just one or two "guest chefs."

MENU

Tossed Salad
Omelettes
French Bread or Crusty Rolls
Cream Cheese Tarts

PARTY POINTERS

- The layered Salad on page 14 would also be good with Omelette Party.

- Prepare all the filling ingredients ahead. Place each in individual bowls, then on a tray for easy transfer to refrigerator and then to table.

- The Cream Cheese Tarts can be frozen after baking and cooling. Add filling and whipped cream before serving.

- Simple crisp cookies would also be a good dessert, page 125-126.

Omelettes

For each omelette, you will need:

- 2 eggs
- 2 teaspoons water
-    dash salt
-    dash pepper
- 1 tablespoon butter or margarine per omelette

Mix enough eggs, water, salt and pepper for your group —
6 guests/12 eggs, etc. Beat all in a large bowl. Use a ¼ cup
ladle to pour egg mixture into frying pan.

Heat a 7″-9″ pan with sloping sides over medium heat. Melt
1 tablespoon of butter in the pan for each omelette cooked.
When the foam begins to subside, ladle out ¼ cup of the
mixture and pour all at once into the cooking pan. As the
edges start to cook, use a spatula to lift the edges so the
liquid portion runs underneath. Shake pan gently to keep
omelette loose. Continue lifting edges until top is no longer
liquid, but still looks moist. Place 2-3 tablespoons filling in
a line down the center of the eggs. Slide the spatula under
one edge of the omelette. Lift and fold over about ⅓ of the
omelette. Slide omelette out of pan so other edge falls over
omelette onto plate covering filling.

Fillings

*Guests select 2-3 fillings. With more than 2-3 tablespoons
of filling, it becomes difficult to cover the fillings with the eggs.
For those with big appetites, make two omelettes with different
fillings.*

green onion, chopped
fresh tomato, chopped
black olives, sliced
avocado, cubed
cooked potato, cubed
green pepper, chopped
mushrooms, sliced —
   raw or lightly sauteed

cooked bacon, crumbled
cooked ham, cubed
shredded cheeses: Cheddar,
   jack, Parmesan
cooked turkey or chicken, cubed
cubed cream cheese

27

Cream Cheese Tarts

A sweet treat that's colorful and easy to serve.

1   package vanilla wafers
1   8-ounce package cream cheese
¼ cup sugar
1   egg
1   teaspoon vanilla
    cherry or blueberry pie filling
½ cup heavy cream, whipped
    paper cupcake liners

Place a vanilla wafer in bottom of each paper-lined, small cupcake pan. Mix room temperature cream cheese with sugar, egg and vanilla. Pour mixture over vanilla wafer. Bake at 350 degrees for 10 minutes. Cool and cover each tart with cherry or blueberry filling. Garnish with whipped cream if desired. Makes 12 tarts.

NOTE: Use the small cupcake pans for recipe.

Pizza Party

Ole solo mio! Everyone is a little Italian when it comes to pizza. For this party, guests make their own unique pizzas using French bread as a base. Add a tossed salad, some red wine, and salutè to a great party.

MENU
Wine
Antipasto Platter
French Bread Pizza
Tossed Salad
Italian Tortoni
Coffee

PARTY POINTERS
- If you don't want to make your own sauce, try a jar of commercial sauce. Ragu Pizza Sauce is very good.
- Plan ¼-½ cup sauce per guest.
- Use purchased marinated vegetables for a quick Antipasto Platter.
- Serve Italian Spumoni Ice Cream for an instant dessert.

Antipasto Platter

This is an easy introduction to an Italian dinner or lunch.

¼   pound broccoli and carrots, cut in chunks
       or strips
¼   pound fresh beans
¼   pound whole, small mushrooms
12 thin sliced salami
12 small slices provolone cheese
3   medium tomatoes, thickly sliced
1   16-ounce can black olives
1   6-ounce can marinated artichoke hearts

In small saucepan place broccoli, carrots, beans and mushrooms. Add ½ cup Italian Salad Dressing. Simmer 5 minutes. Cool. Then refrigerate several hours or overnight.

Arrange antipasto ingredients on a large platter in an attractive display. Drizzle reserved artichoke marinade over tomatoes. Serves 8.

Tossed Salad

A nice, crisp and ever popular accompaniment to pizza.

1 large head Romaine lettuce
1 bunch green onions
2 medium tomatoes
1 16-ounce can pitted black olives
    Good Seasons Italian Dressing, mixed

Wash and dry lettuce. Place in plastic bag with damp paper towels. It will keep several days. Chop green onions and slice tomatoes. You may store onions and tomatoes in small plastic bags in the refrigerator overnight.

If doing salad ahead, place the lettuce in a plastic bag with a dampened paper towel; close bag and refrigerate. Before guests arrive, place the lettuce in a large bowl and sprinkle green onions and olives. Add tomatoes and toss with dressing just before serving.

Dressing

Good Seasons makes a good Italian dressing. To make it special, add ¼ cup grated Parmesan cheese.

French Bread Base and Toppings

Plan to use one whole poor boy roll, or French dip sandwich roll per person, with a few extras for those with hearty appetites. Dry bread by heating in a 200 degree oven for 15 minutes. This will prevent a soggy crust. Brush the top of the bread with melted butter. Arrange bread in a basket. Each guest places the bread on a plate and goes Italian with any, or if adventurous, a wide variety of the following toppings:

½-1 pound mushrooms, sauteed in 1-2
    tablespoons olive oil
2 large onions, sauteed in 2 tablespoons olive oil
black olives, sliced
green olives, sliced
green onions, chopped
green pepper, sliced or chopped
fresh tomatoes, sliced
pepperoni, sliced
ham, shredded
pineapple tidbits
anchovies
small shrimp
cooked ground beef, crumbled
Cheddar cheese, shredded
Monterey jack or mozzarella cheese
French bread or French rolls cut in half lengthwise
tomato sauce

NOTE: If using French bread, cut in half lengthwise. Then cut each half into 3 pieces. Allow 2 or 3 pieces per guest.

Quick Pizza Tomato Sauce

A day in the refrigerator helps the flavors to "marry," — a good do-ahead feature.

2 tablespoons olive oil
1 large onion, coarsely chopped
2 cloves garlic, minced
1 1 pound, 3-ounce can whole tomatoes
2 8-ounce tomato sauce
1 teaspoon dried oregano, crushed
1 teaspoon sugar
1 teaspoon salt
  dash of pepper

In a 2 quart saucepan saute onion and garlic until onion is clear. Drain tomatoes, reserving liquid. Mash tomatoes. Add to onion and garlic. Add reserved liquid, tomato sauce, dried oregano, sugar, salt and pepper. Simmer about 30 minutes, stirring occasionally. Makes 3 cups; enough for 6-8 guests.

To Bake French Bread Pizzas

Once guests have created their pizzas using a layer of tomato sauce and then toppings ending with cheese, bake them on a cookie sheet in a 375 degree oven about 20 minutes or until cheese is hot and bubbly.

Italian Tortoni

Individual servings of a creamy custard, flavored with almond.

3 egg yolks
¾ cup confectioners' sugar
3 tablespoons sherry or Amaretto liqueur
½ teaspoon vanilla extract
¼ teaspoon almond extract if using sherry above
3 egg whites
1½ cups heavy cream, whipped
1½ cups coconut macaroons, crushed

32

In a small mixing bowl, beat egg yolks and sugar until light and fluffy. Add sherry or Amaretto and vanilla, mixing well. In another bowl, beat egg whites until stiff, but not dry. Carefully fold egg yolk mixture into whites. Then fold in whipped cream until all is well combined. Gently stir in ¾ cup crushed macaroons. Pour into 10-12 paper liners placed in cupcake pans. Sprinkle remaining crumbs on top. Can be made 2 days ahead and refrigerated or frozen for longer storage. Makes 10-12.

Variations:

At Christmas time decorate top with red and green cherry poinsettia. Cut small piece of green for center of flower. Cut 2 red halves into 4 "petals" each. Arrange petals in spoke fashion around center.

Pretzel Party

Teens really enjoy this make-your-own Pretzel Party. It's also a great one for that difficult-to-please group — pre-teens. And of course, adults and children enjoy it, too. Gather everyone around the kitchen table to twist frozen bread dough into pretzel shapes. While waiting for the pretzels to bake, guests could play table games or sing carols around the Christmas tree during the holiday season.

MENU
Pretzels
Coarse Salt, Poppyseeds, Sesame Seeds
Cold Cider
Hot Cider
or
Hot Chocolate

PARTY POINTERS
- Be sure to have some finished samples for guests to copy.
- You'll need a place where guests can shape their pretzels — a counter area or a table with flour handy.
- Sometimes children don't like the coarse salt, so use a little regular salt instead.
- Each guest may want his own pretzel, especially when children are guests. Let each person write his or her name on the foil next to the pretzel, so it can be recognized as it comes out of the oven.

Pretzels

Use a basic bread dough recipe if you prefer. For the frozen dough, simply thaw, lightly butter and cover it with a kitchen towel to keep it from drying out.

2 1-pound loaves frozen bread dough (1 loaf
   per 4-5 guests)
2 eggs, beaten
   coarse salt
   sesame seeds
   poppy seeds
   one or two pastry brushes, or new 1" paint brushes
    from the hardware store
   aluminum foil
   cookie sheets

For each pretzel, cut off a golf-ball size piece of dough. Roll into a rope about 16" long. Twist to form regular pretzel shape. Lightly grease several foil-lined cookie sheets. Place twisted pretzels on sheet; brush with beaten eggs and sprinkle with salt or seeds. Allow to rest 15 minutes if possible, then bake at 450 degrees for 12-15 minutes. Pretzels should be golden brown when done.

Offer mustard to spread on warm pretzels.

Salad Bar Party

Fresh salad bars are now a popular part of many restaurants' menus. Why not use the idea for a party to please everyone from the dainty dieter to the hearty eater? Dinner can be as light or as abundant as a guest chooses. Crunchy French bread compliments the meal, and a beautiful layered Trifle tops it off as dessert.

MENU
Wine
Sausage Balls, page 110
Chicken Wings, page 112
Salad Bar
Bread/Bread Sticks/Crackers
Trifle, page 59

PARTY POINTERS
- Summer is the perfect time for this party. Try serving it outside in the yard or on the deck.
- This could be a taco salad party by using seasoned hamburger, cheeses, tomato, avocado and taco chips.
- Serve salad dressing from small pitchers, gravy boats or small bowls with ladles.
- Chill the salad plates for a special touch.
- This could easily be a luncheon party.

Salad Bar

This is enough for 8-12 people.

2   large heads of lettuce, torn into
        bite size pieces
2   bunches spinach leaves, torn into
        bite size pieces
½   cup pickled beets
1   cup garbanzo beans
1½   cups cooked chicken or turkey, cubed
        bacon, crumbled
1½   cups ham, cubed
1½   cups turkey
1   pint alfalfa sprouts
1   cup marinated green beans
1   cup croutons
½   cup Parmesan cheese
1   cup Cheddar cheese
½   cup sunflower seeds
½   cup peanuts
        Mama's Avocado dressing
        Good Seasons Creamy Blue Cheese dressing mix
        Good Seasons French dressing mix

Arrange a large bowl of broken lettuce and a smaller one of spinach leaves. Place all the other ingredients in small bowls with spoons for self service. Arrange dressings at end of salad bar.

Place bread in napkin lined basket and stand breadsticks up in another basket.

Offer some of the fancy crackers such as Waverly crackers.

Variation:
Serve Pita Points, page 88.

Mama's Avocado Salad Dressing

Garlicy and tangy with a creamy avocado flavor. Make dressing in food processor or blender.

2   cloves garlic
1   cup oil
1   teaspoon dry mustard
½   cup vinegar
1   teaspoon salt
1   teaspoon Italian Seasonings
¼   teaspoon black pepper
1   teaspoon sugar
½   cup water
    a pinch of oregano
1   small or ½ of a large avocado

Turn processor on and drop in garlic. Add oil, dry mustard, vinegar, salt, Italian Seasonings, pepper, sugar, water and oregano. Process about 1 minute. Add avocado and process 30 seconds more. Makes 1½ cups.

Cheese Bread, page 41 or **Parmesan Bread Ring**, page 41
Trifle, page 59

Soup Party

There's something homey and comforting about soup — it's friendly. This party is a sure winner on a cold day. Or why not use a cold gazpacho recipe in the summer? Each guest contributes by bringing one item for the soup — tomatoes, celery, potatoes, onions, turnips, carrots, etc. The host or hostess prepares a tasty chicken or beef stock and the vegetables are added according to the amount of time they require to be cooked.

MENU

Wine
Cheese and Crackers
Vickie's Vegetable Soup
Garnishes
Cheese Bread/Parmesan Bread Ring
Mud Pie

PARTY POINTERS

- The host or hostess prepares the browned beef and guests add their items. Cover and simmer as everyone enjoys a glass of wine and some crackers and cheese.
- With large crowds, make several pots of soup for faster cooking.
- Prepare cheese bread the night before and refrigerate.
- Serve soup from a crock pot to keep it hot for several hours.
- Use a dinner plate with a cup or mug for easier buffet

service. Guests then have room for bread on plate.
- You could add a salad to this menu. Try Layered Salad, page 14. Or Oriental Salad, page 95-96.

Vickie's Vegetable Soup

A hearty, homestyle soup everyone loves.

1 pound ground beef
1 or 2 tablespoons fat
1 cup chopped onion
4 cups hot water or bouillon
1 bay leaf
  pinch of basil
6 whole tomatoes
1 cup each: chopped carrots, celery, potatoes
2 teaspoons salt
½ teaspoon pepper
1 teaspoon Worcestershire sauce

Brown beef in hot fat in heavy kettle. Add onions and cook about 5 minutes. Add water (or bouillon). As guests arrive, add carrots, celery, potatoes and seasonings. Mix thoroughly. Bring to boil. Cover and simmer about 30 minutes or as long as needed. Arrange soup bowls, spoons and napkins on buffet table. Place following items in containers on table and let guests garnish their own soup:

Garnishes

Parmesan cheese
grated Cheddar cheese
small soup crackers (oyster crackers or the
  little fish made by Pepperidge Farms)
croutons
sour cream

Cheese Bread

A crunchy accompaniment to any soup, this bread is not for calorie counters, but it's worth going off your diet to try.

2　cups grated sharp Cheddar cheese
½　cup mayonnaise or enough to moisten
　　　cheese to spreading consistency
1　bunch green onions, chopped
1　loaf French bread, sliced in half lengthwise

Mix grated cheese, mayonnaise and green onion. Spread thickly on both halves of bread. Wrap in foil and bake in 400 degree oven for 20 minutes. Open the foil and turn oven to broil. Watch carefully until cheese bubbles, then remove and cut into pieces. Serve hot.

NOTE: Bread can be prepared 24 hours in advance and refrigerated. Just bake and broil before serving.

Parmesan Bread Ring

Serve this hot from the oven. Guests help themselves by tearing off each crusty roll.

2　loaves frozen white bread dough
½　cup melted butter or margarine
½　cup grated Parmesan cheese

Thaw dough according to package directions. Cut each loaf into 13 pieces, and dip each piece into the melted butter. Next dip in Parmesan cheese and stack dipped pieces, two or three deep, in a greased bundt or angel food cake pan. Cover with a clean kitchen towel and allow to rise until about double in size (around an hour). Bake at 350 degrees for 30-35 minutes or until loaf is golden brown and sounds hollow when tapped.

Mud Pie

24   Oreo cookies, or use 18 cookies and ½ cup cornflake crumbs. Crush cookies in food processor or put in ziplock bag and crush with a rolling pin
½   cup nuts, chopped
1   stick butter or margarine
½   gallon mocha ice cream
1   16-ounce jar chocolate syrup
1   cup heavy cream, whipped with
¼   cup powdered sugar and
1   teaspoon vanilla
9″   square pan

Remove ice cream from freezer so it will be soft enough to spread. Crush cookie crumbs. Reserve ½ cup for top. Mix butter with crumbs and nuts and press into bottom of pan. Spread softened ice cream over syrup. Cover ice cream with a second layer of syrup. Cover and freeze. When ready to serve cut into squares and place a dollop of whipping cream on each serving.

Spud Party

Americans love baked potatoes filled with tasty toppings, and this party is a potato lover's dream. Each guest selects one or more steaming hot baked potatoes and fills them with anything from sour cream to chipped beef. A fresh green salad, white wine and apple cobbler for dessert complete an unusual party, perfect for just a few friends or a big crowd.

MENU
Wine
Appetizer Bouquet
Tossed Salad
Baked Potatoes
Potato Toppings
Apple-Walnut Cobbler

PARTY POINTERS
- Use scissors to cut green onions.
- Select firm, blemish-free baking potatoes.
- Avoid any green tint on potatoes. This will cause them to taste bitter.
- Do not store potatoes in the refrigerator, or they will taste sweet. Store them in a cool, dry place.
- Cut potatoes in half lengthwise and offer 2-3 halves to each person. Guests can try a variety of toppings this way.

- Wash potatoes and have them ready to pop in the oven 1 hour before your guests arrive.

Appetizer Bouquet

Hors d'oeuvres are skewered with wooden skewers or toothpicks and then pushed into a parsley covered loaf of French bread. It's so pretty you can use it as a centerpiece.

Amounts of each ingredient are not important.

 1 ounce can whole mushrooms, or small fresh mushrooms
 1 dry pint cherry tomatoes
 1 ounce can giant, pitted olives
 1 ounce can green olives
 ½ pound jack cheese, cut into 1" cubes
 ½ pound Cheddar cheese, cut into 1" cubes
 1 package small bread sticks
 1 jar midget dill pickles
 1 jar midget sweet pickles
 1 round or long loaf French type bread
   fresh parsley

Cover top and sides of bread with parsley, holding pieces in place with toothpicks. Skewer all the items with wooden skewers or toothpicks and arrange over the entire loaf of covered bread. This is most attractive if skewers are of different heights on the bread. Serve on a plate or on shallow basket.

Variations:

You could add some of the vegetable cut outs on page 115.

Add cubes of salami, sausage or cooked ham or any other ingredient you can easily skewer, such as broccoli and cauliflower flowerettes, marinated vegetables, cocktail onions.

Baked Potatoes

To serve potatoes, arrange on parsley covered platter with whole cherry tomatoes or sliced tomatoes for garnish.

Baking Potatoes, 2-3 per guest

Bake medium to large potatoes in a 400 degree oven for 45 minutes to an hour. You might want to use potato nails — sold in kitchen gadget department — but do not wrap potatoes in foil, or skins will be soft. HINT: Speed up baking time with a microwave oven. Potatoes take only minutes when cooked this way. Follow oven directions.

Potato Toppings

Place each of the following in a small bowl and arrange on a buffet table. Amounts given will serve 6-8 people.

½ pound (1 cup) butter
1 pint (2 cups) sour cream
1 bunch green onions, chopped
4 medium (2 cups) fresh tomato, chopped
1 cup Cheddar cheese, shredded
1 pound bacon — cooked, drained and crumbled
2 cups ham, slivered
2-3 cups creamed chipped beef
2 cups chili, canned without beans or homemade, page 128
2 cups guacamole

Each of these toppings can be prepared ahead of time. Place sour cream in bowl and cover. Chop green onions, and tomatoes. Grate and shred cheese. Cook, drain and crumble bacon and cut ham into fine strips 2 inches long. Place each item in a separate ziplock bag and refrigerate overnight, if desired. Make a white sauce, page 76, and add three 2-ounce packages of chipped beef cut into strips. Reheat in a double boiler or in microwave oven.

Apple-Walnut Cobbler

This is truly delicious served warm.

4   cups thinly sliced tart apples
½   cup sugar
½   teaspoon cinnamon, more if you like cinnamon
    walnuts, coarsely chopped

1   cup sugar
1   cup sifted flour
¼   teaspoon baking powder
1   well-beaten egg
½   cup evaporated milk
⅓   cup melted butter
    whipped cream or ice cream
    8" x 8" baking dish

Spread apple slices over bottom of well-greased 8" x 8" baking dish. In a small bowl, mix ½ cup sugar, cinnamon and walnuts. Pour mixture over apples. Mix 1 cup sugar, flour, salt and baking powder. Add egg, milk and butter; mix. Pour over apples. Sprinkle with ¼ cup walnuts. Bake approximately 45-55 minutes at 325-350 degrees or until golden brown. Serve with whipped cream or ice cream. Serves 4-6. Double recipe for 9" x 13" pan to serve 10-12.

Stewpendous

Guests assemble individual do-it-yourself stews, choosing from mini meatballs, sausages, weiners, carrots, onions, potatoes, mushrooms, corn and peas. A delicious gravy is poured over all and it is heated in the oven until bubbly hot. Crisp and tangy cheese bread and a strawberry pie top this hearty lunch or dinner fare.

MENU
Wine
Cheese and Crackers
Salad
Stewpendous
Old English French Bread
Mile High Strawberry Pie

PARTY POINTERS
- Prepare the meatballs a day or two ahead or make them weeks ahead and freeze.
- Steam the potatoes and carrots the day ahead.
- Use oven proof bowls or small casseroles to hold stew. Or for a large group you might use small aluminum mini loaf pans.
- Tell guests to fill casseroles or pans about ½ full and then cover meat and vegetables with sauce.
- This would make a good outdoor party or even a picnic. Wrap aluminum pans in foil and heat 6″ above coals until hot, 20-30 minutes.

Stewpendous

A meal in one.

2   lbs. Mini-Meatballs (recipe follows)
1   lb. sausage, Polish, Kasaba or German, cut
       into 1" chunks
1   lb. dinner franks, cut into 1" chunks
1½   lbs. potatoes, cut in chunks and steamed
1   lb. onions, steamed until just limp
1   lb. carrots, sliced paper thin or cut into
       chunks and steamed
1   bunch celery, thinly sliced
2   8-ounce cans, whole button mushrooms
1   10-ounce package frozen corn
1   10-ounce package frozen peas
     Gravy (recipe follows)

Arrange all ingredients in separate containers. Guests heap chosen ingredients in oven proof containers. Bake in 350 degree oven for 20-30 minutes. Longer baking time won't hurt stew.

Mini-Meatballs

2   lbs. lean ground beef
2   eggs, slightly beaten
½   cup seasoned Italian bread crumbs
1   teaspoon soy sauce

Mix meat, eggs, bread crumbs and soy sauce. Shape into ½" balls. Place on rimmed cookie sheet and bake at 450 degrees about 5 minutes. Remove from sheet, cover and refrigerate or freeze.

Gravy

A simple sauce that takes on the flavor of all the stew ingredients.

2 8-ounce cans tomato sauce
2 14-ounce cans cream of mushroom soup
1 14-ounce can beef broth
1 teaspoon bottled steak or Worcestershire sauce

Simmer soups and broth together for 15 minutes. Pour into pitcher or small soup tureen with ladle.

Old English French Bread

1 loaf French bread
1 cup butter, softened
1 jar Old English cheese spread

Cut loaf into slices. Spread each slice first with butter, then with cheese spread, or mix butter and cheese spread in food processor until smooth, then spread. Wrap well in foil and refrigerate up to 2 days or freeze for longer storage. To serve, place wrapped bread in 400 degree oven about 15 minutes. Serve hot. OR **Cheese Bread,** page 41.

Mile High Strawberry Pie

A light and fluffy pink cloud.

1 10-ounce package frozen sweetened strawberries, thawed
2 egg whites
½ cup sugar
1 tablespoon lemon juice
1 pint heavy cream, whipped
1 8″ or 9″ graham cracker or pastry pie shell
1 cup whipping cream, whipped, sweetened and flavored with 1 teaspoon almond extract
¼ cup slivered almonds

In the large bowl of an electric mixer place strawberries and egg whites. Turn mixer on high and beat 15 minutes. Mixture will rise to the top of the bowl. Carefully fold whipped cream into strawberry mixture. Pour into pie shell and freeze. Remove from freezer 15 minutes before serving. Serve with dollops of whipped cream and sprinkle with almonds.

Sundae Party

Watch the "little kid" come out in your guests as they gaze at a table laden with creamy ice cream and a variety of soda-shop toppings. Everyone piles up their own combination of sauces, nuts and whipped cream to make his or her own sundae — don't forget the maraschino cherries to make each sundae picture perfect.

MENU
Ice Cream
Chocolate Fudge Topping, purchased
Butterscotch Topping
Strawberry Topping, purchased
Crushed Pineapple Topping
Marshmallow Creme
Whipped Cream
Crunchy Toffee Topping
Chopped Nuts

PARTY POINTERS
- To help keep ice cream from melting while serving, place ice cream balls in chilled glass or metal bowls. Fill a second larger, chilled bowl with ice cubes or crushed ice and set the first bowl in the ice-filled second bowl.

- Each ½ gallon of ice cream will make about 15 ice cream balls. Each quart makes about 8.

- Instead of piling ice cream balls in a bowl, scoop ice cream balls and place in paper muffin liners. Cover well with foil and freeze for up to 24 hours. Place the ice cream liners on a platter to serve.

- If time is of the essence, look for commercial ice cream toppings at your local grocery store. Most are very good.
- Allow 4-6 tablespoons each of sauce and toppings for each person.
- Use fondue pots to keep toppings warm.
- You'll need 1 pint of whipping cream, whipped, for every 10 guests.

Ice Cream Balls

1 gallon ice cream
ice cream scoop
small bowl of warm water
waxed paper
cookie sheet
ziplock bags

Set ice cream out of freezer for about 15 minutes. Cover cookie sheet with waxed paper. Dip ice cream scoop into bowl of warm water. Scoop ice cream aand place 2 inches apart on wax paper-covered cookie sheet. Place in freezer until balls are frozen hard. Place balls in ziplock bags. They will keep 3-4 days.

Chocolate Fudge Topping

Smucker's or Hershey's makes a devilishly fudgy topping. Simply heat and pour into a small pitcher for serving.

Chocolate Shot

Buy the small bottles of chocolate shot in the baking section of your grocery store, or use mini chocolate chips or grated chocolate.

Butterscotch Topping

   1 6-ounce package butterscotch chips
   1 cup heavy cream

In a small saucepan heat cream and chips. Stir until chips are melted. Serve warm. Makes about 1½ cups.

Crushed Pineapple Topping

   1 15-ounce can crushed pineapple in light syrup
  ½ cup light corn syrup
   1 tablespoon cornstarch
   1 tablespoon cold water

Drain pineapple syrup into small saucepan. Add corn syrup. Heat to boiling. Mix cornstarch with water until smooth. Add hot syrups and simmer just until thick. Add crushed pineapple. Makes 2 cups. Serve warm or cold.

Marshmallow Creme

Place a 7-ounce jar of marshmallow creme in a pan of hot water for 10 minutes, or remove cover and heat in microwave on low power about 10 seconds. Using a spoon dipped in hot water, spoon out cream into bowl. Serve.

Crunchy Toffee Topping

Break up 4 3½-ounce Heath bars into small pieces. Place in a small bowl to be sprinkled over ice cream.

Chopped Nuts

Offer one or two types of chopped nuts. Walnuts and almonds are the most popular. Toast them in a 325 degree oven for 10 minutes before serving. A half cup of each is enough for 8-10 guests.

Variation:

- Roll some of the ice cream balls in coconut or in chocolate shot.
- Coconut is another topping possibility.

"Waf'ly Good" Waffle Party

Here's a great after-church party, perfect for family gatherings, too. Crisp light waffles are the star attraction. Then guests go creative with toppings of fruit, whipped cream or syrups. Add sausage, ham or bacon and piping hot coffee and it's a delightful way to start the day.

❦

MENU
Apricot Cooler
Wonderful Waffles
Toppings
Blueberry and Maple Orange Syrups
Do-Ahead Sausages
Bacon for a Crowd
Coffee

PARTY POINTERS
- Borrow one or two waffle irons if you're expecting a crowd.
- Arrange all the fixings on a buffet table and let guests create their own waffles.
- Let guests bake their own waffles, too, or assign that task to one person.
- Be sure waffle iron is very hot. Test by sprinkling a drop of water on it. If water bounces, it is ready.
- A pitcher makes it easy to pour batter onto iron.
- Pour batter around center of iron. Fill only ¾ full to avoid overflow.

- Store leftover batter in covered container in refrigerator. It will keep up to 3 days.

Apricot Cooler

 1 46-ounce can apricot nectar
 1 6-ounce can orange juice concentrate
 1 28-ounce bottle 7-Up or gingerale

In a large pitcher or punch bowl, mix apricot nectar and orange juice concentrate. This can be done early in the day and refrigerated. Just before serving, add 7-Up or gingerale.

Garnishes: Slice oranges and float on top of cooler if using a punch bowl, or make a slit to the center of each orange slice and hang on the side of each glass for individual servings. A sprig of mint at the side of the glass is a nice touch.

Waffles

Crisp on the outside, soft on the inside and light as air.

 2 cups sifted flour
 3 teaspoons baking powder
 2 tablespoons sugar
 1 teaspoon salt
 3 egg yolks, beaten
 3 egg whites, beaten until stiff
 1¼ cups milk
 4 tablespoons melted shortening

Sift flour, baking powder, sugar and salt into medium bowl. Mix beaten egg yolks, milk and shortening. Beat thoroughly.

Add to dry ingredients, stirring lightly until mixed. Fold in beaten egg whites gently. Bake 3-4 minutes in a hot waffle iron. Makes 5-6 waffles.

Waffle Variations:

- Apple waffles. Add 1 teaspoon cinnamon with dry ingredients. Add 1 cup chopped raw apple to batter. Serve with cinnomon and sugar and butter. Serve with orange maple syrup.

- Blueberry waffles. Add 1 cup fresh or frozen blueberries to dry ingredients. A half teaspoon cinnamon is a nice flavor accent. Serve with blueberry syrup.

- Chocolate waffles. Add ½ cup cocoa and increase sugar to ¼ cup. Sift with dry ingredients. Serve with whipped cream.

- Nut waffles. Add 2 tablespoons of chopped nuts to dry ingredients. Serve with orange maple syrup.

- Orange waffles. Add 1 tablespoon grated orange rind to batter and substitute ½ cup orange juice for ½ cup milk. Serve with orange maple syrup.

Quick Blueberry Sauce

1 14½-ounce can blueberries
3 tablespoons light corn syrup
dash of cinnamon
dash of nutmeg

Drain blueberries. Heat blueberry liquid in a small saucepan. Add corn syrup. Simmer mixture over medium heat stirring occasionally, 8-10 minutes. Add blueberries and serve warm. Makes 2 cups.

Orange Maple Syrup

2 cups maple-flavored syrup
1 cup butter or margarine
1½ teaspoons grated orange peel
2 teaspoons orange liqueur (optional)

In a small saucepan heat syrup, butter, orange peel and liqueur, 5 minutes. Serve warm. Makes 3 cups.

Toppings

whipped cream
chopped walnuts, almonds or pecans
warm applesauce, especially good on
    Apple Waffle
sliced strawberries

Do-Ahead Sausages

In a large skillet place links with ¼ cup water. Cover and steam about 5 minutes. Drain and refrigerate up to 24 hours. When ready to cook and serve, place sausages on rack over pan and bake at 350 degrees 10 minutes or until done.

Bacon for a Crowd

Baked bacon is easy and perfect when preparing a large amount. Place unseparated bacon on the rack of a broiler pan or on cake racks over jelly roll pans. Bake at 400 degrees 5 minutes. Separate bacon into strips. Bake 15 more minutes. No turning is necessary. Drain on several thicknesses of paper toweling and serve.

Dessert Parties

Dessert Party Buffet

My husband's family had a wonderful bakery in Portland for years. People came from miles away just to buy Pop Bauer's butterhorns, eclairs and chess pies. Naturally, a sweet tooth runs in the family and this party is one of my husband's favorites. You may want to substitute your own famous and favorite desserts, but no matter how you present it, this party is a hit. Three or four items are plenty, with at least one item being chocolate. Serve a good quality coffee, or if you're feeling "flush" as they say, serve champagne! Of course, if you have chocolate loving friends, then the all-chocolate party is the one to plan. It's devilishly delicious.

MENU
Trifle
Assorted Cookies
Chocolate Fondue and Fresh Fruit, page 25
Coffee/Champagne

PARTY POINTERS
- Use a deep clear glass bowl for trifle so the layers are seen.
- Serve trifle in small glass bowls rather than on plates.

Trifle

A beautiful dessert served in a large glass bowl. The recipe is easy to expand for a larger bowl and group.

2	pound cakes, frozen or bakery variety
1	3½-ounce package vanilla instant pudding mix
1½	cups milk
¼	cup Sherry or Liqueur, for cake
1	pint whipping cream, whipped
15½	ounce Smucker's low sugar Raspberry spread
1	cup almonds, slivered
½	cup heavy cream, whipped, sweetened for garnish

In a medium-size bowl or in a food processor mix instant pudding, milk and liqueur. Fold whipped cream into pudding mixture. Cut pound cakes into ½" slices. Spread each slice with raspberry spread. Place a layer of cake in a medium-size, clear glass bowl. Drizzle with sherry or liqueur. Cover with layer of ⅓ pudding mixture. Repeat cake, sherry, pudding for three layers. Garnish with whipped cream and sprinkle with ⅓ cup nuts. Refrigerate up to 24 hours.

Variations:

- Make an unusual trifle using chocolate pudding in place of vanilla and Coffee Liqueur to drizzle over cake. Garnish with whipping cream and shaved chocolate and almonds.

Assorted Cookies

Unless you have some cookies tucked away in the freezer, simply buy some Pepperidge Farm or some of the new fancy Nabisco varieties, or try a bakery. Arrange on a doily-lined tray or a tiered server.

Other Dessert Ideas

Truffles, page 18
Mile High Strawberry Pie, page 49
Cream Puffs, page 61
Cranberry Mousse, page 90
Apple Walnut Cobbler, page 46
Mud Pie, page 42
Nut Clusters, page 19

The Real Chocolate-Lover's Dessert Party

This is a chocoholic's dream.

MENU
Chocolate Cream Puffs
Chocolate Mocha Mousse in Chocolate Cups
German Sweet Chocolate Pie
Chocolate Fondue
Truffles

PARTY POINTERS
- The Chocolate Party is nearly all do-ahead.
- With a buffet service such as this, it's important that all items will hold up well for a time in case guests return to the table.
- Note that this party is not inexpensive to create, but compared to a full meal, it's most affordable and truly memorable.

Chocolate Cream Puffs

Make the puffs weeks ahead and freeze them, then fill them several hours before serving. These are made two-bite size so guests can sample several desserts, but if you serve this as a single dessert make the puffs bigger. Place each puff in a cupcake paper liner to serve.

1   cup water
½   cup butter or margarine
1   cup all purpose flour
¼   teaspoon salt
4   large eggs
    Chocolate Whipped Cream Filling (recipe follows)
    Chocolate Glaze (recipe follows)

Preheat oven to 400 degrees. In a medium-size saucepan bring water, butter and salt to a boil. Remove from heat. Using a wooden spoon, beat in the flour all at once. Return to low heat and continue beating about 1 minute. Remove from heat again and beat in eggs one at a time until mixture is smooth. Continue beating until dough is shiny and satiny. It will break into strands.

Drop mixture by tablespoons onto ungreased cookie sheet, about 2" apart. Bake 45-50 minutes until dry, puffed and golden. Puffs will sound hollow when tapped. Cool on wire racks.

(For smaller puffs, reduce temperature to 375 degrees and bake until light brown.) Cut puffs ⅓ of the way from top. Pull out doughy pieces inside. Flash freeze puffs on cookie sheets and then wrap well for freezer storage. They will keep in freezer for 3-4 weeks. To serve, fill with Chocolate Whipped Cream and frost with Chocolate Glaze.

Chocolate Whipped Cream

1   pint (2 cups) heavy cream
3   tablespoons cocoa
¼   cup powdered sugar

61

In a chilled bowl place whipping cream, cocoa, and powdered sugar. Whip until very stiff. Use to fill cream puffs.

Chocolate Glaze

1 cup chocolate chips
2 tablespoons shortening (Crisco)
2 tablespoons white corn syrup
3 tablespoons milk

In a double boiler or in microwave oven, melt chocolate and shortening. Add corn syrup and milk. Stir until smooth. Cool slightly. Place filled cream puffs on wire rack with waxed paper underneath. Pour warm glaze over puffs. Refrigerate up to 4 hours.

Chocolate Cups

Make these delicious containers in the mini cupcake liners to fill with Mocha Mousse or liqueur and drop into hot coffee. Or make them in a standard cupcake liner and fill with ice cream for an individual dessert.

To make cups use:

12-ounces semisweet chocolate chips
paper cupcake liners

In the top of a double boiler or in a glass bowl in a microwave, melt chocolate chips. Using the back of a spoon or a pastry brush, coat the inside of cupcake liners, placed in muffin tins, until about ¼" thick with chocolate. Place muffin tins on cookie sheet and refrigerate 30 minutes to harden cups. Peel off paper. Cover cups with plastic wrap and refrigerate up to 2 days, or wrap well and freeze in a box to avoid breaking. Makes 8 standard cups or 16 mini cups.

To serve mini cups with coffee:

• Fill with sweetened whipped cream.

- Fill with Chocolate Mocha Mousse.
- Fill with liqueur.

Float filled chocolate cup in steaming coffee. Guests stir and enjoy.

To serve standard sized chocolate cup as dessert, fill each with:

- Chocolate ice cream topped with crumbled Oreos.
- Mocha ice cream topped with slivered, toasted almonds.
- Vanilla ice cream sprinkled with instant coffee granules.
- Chocolate Mocha Mousse.

Chocolate Mocha Mousse

Sinfully delicious! A wonderful filling for dessert crepes or chocolate cups, or serve alone in a stemmed glass with crisp cookies.

6 ounces (1 cup) chocolate chips
¼ cup double strength coffee (use instant or add
      1 teaspoon instant to ¼ cup coffee) or espresso
3 egg yolks
½ pint heavy cream
¼ cup powdered sugar
1 teaspoon vanilla extract, or 1 tablespoon coffee
      liqueur, recipe on page 173-175

In the top of a double boiler or in a microwave oven, melt chocolate with coffee. Beat egg yolks, and whisk into chocolate. Add vanilla or liqueur.

In a well chilled bowl beat cream and powdered sugar until very stiff. Fold into chocolate mixture. Refrigerate several hours. Use to fill mini or standard size chocolate cups (recipe follows). Top with whipped cream and shaved or chopped chocolate. Makes 1½ cups mousse. Enough to fill 12 standard size chocolate cups.

German Sweet Chocolate Pie

Watch for sales on cream cheese and Cool Whip and have them on hand in your freezer for this recipe.

1	package (4 ounces) Baker's German Sweet Chocolate
⅓	cup Coffee Liqueur
2	tablespoons sugar
1	package (3 ounces) cream cheese, softened
3½	cups (8-ounce container) Cool Whip, thawed, or 1 pint heavy cream, whipped
8"	graham cracker crumb crust
½	cup heavy cream, whipped chocolate bar

Heat chocolate and 2 tablespoons of the milk in a saucepan over low heat, stirring until chocolate is melted. Beat sugar into cream cheese; add liqueur and chocolate mixture and beat until smooth. Fold in whipped topping, until smooth. Spoon into crust. Freeze until firm. Garnish with dollops of whipped cream and shaved chocolate. Makes one 8" pie.

Chocolate Fondue
See page 25

Chocolate Truffles
See page 18

Bunch of Brunches

Brunches

If I had to choose my favorite form of entertaining, it would be a Sunday Brunch. It's such a relaxed time of the week. No one is rushed or tired. It's just a joy to share a midday meal.

Preparation can be as simple or elaborate as the mood moves you and time allows. Nearly all the preparation can be done a day ahead leaving you rested and ready to enjoy time with special friends.

MENU I

Easy
Orange Juliette
Creamy Egg Brunch Dish
Six-Week Bran Muffins
Strawberry Butter

MENU II

Easier
Curried Fruit
Quick Quiche
Blueberry Cinnamon Muffins

MENU III

Easiest
Fresh Fruit Plate
with Hawaiian Bananas
Sausage Puff
Coffee Cake

MENU IV

Simply Elegant
Fruit Compote
Curried Ham and Chicken Crepes
Kringla

PARTY POINTERS
- If you'd like to serve a dessert with any of the menus, choose any one of the following:

Grasshopper Pie, page 86-87
Mile High Strawberry Pie, page 49
Apple Walnut Cobbler, page 46
Chocolate Mousse in Chocolate Cups, page 62-63
Cream Puffs, page 6
German Sweet Chocolate Pie, page 64

- Champagne or white wine are always perfect with any brunch, or simply serve a fruit juice drink or punch.

Brunch Menu I

Easy
Orange Juliette
Creamy Egg Brunch Dish
Six-Week Bran Muffins
Strawberry Butter

Orange Juliette

Frosty, tasty and nutritious

1   6-ounce can frozen orange juice concentrate
1   cup milk
½   cup water
½   cup sugar
1   teaspoon vanilla
6-9 ice cubes

In blender or food processor, combine juice concentrate, milk, water, sugar, vanilla and ice cubes. Cover and blend 15-30 seconds. Pour into glasses and serve immediately. Makes about 6 cups.

Creamy Egg Brunch Dish

A velvety white sauce is richly flavored with bacon and chipped beef. Then scrambled eggs and mushrooms are layered and smothered with sauce making this a memorable do-ahead meal.

6-8 slices bacon, cut into 1″ pieces
8 ounces dried beef, cut into 1″ strips
2 4-ounce cans sliced mushrooms (one can for sauce and one can for top of finished dish)
¼ cup butter
½ cup flour
1 quart milk (whole or 2 percent)
 dash of pepper
16 eggs
¼ teaspoon salt
1 cup evaporated milk
¼ cup butter

In a large frying pan, saute cut bacon. Add cut dried beef, one can mushrooms and ¼ cup butter. When butter sizzles add flour, stirring until blended. Add milk, stirring until sauce is smooth and thick. Set sauce aside.

In a medium bowl, beat eggs with salt and evaporated milk. In another large frying pan melt butter; when butter sizzles, add eggs and scramble, keeping eggs creamy rather than dry.

Butter a 9″ x 13″ pan. Pour enough sauce in pan to cover the bottom. Layer as follows: scrambled eggs, sauce, eggs, sauce and garnish top with second can of drained mushrooms.

Bake uncovered 1 hour at 275 degrees, or cover and refrigerate 24 hours, bring to room temperature and bake.

Six-Week Bran Muffins

Hot steaming muffins with melting butter are a morning dream. You can make dreams come true any morning with this muffin batter in your refrigerator.

3   cups whole bran cereal
1   cup boiling water
2   eggs, slightly beaten
2   cups buttermilk
½   cup salad oil
1   cup raisins,* chopped apple, dates or nuts
2½ teaspoons soda
½   teaspoon salt
½   sugar
2   tablespoons molasses (optional)
2½ cups regular all purpose flour unsifted

In a large bowl mix cereal with water, stirring to moisten evenly. Set aside until cool — add eggs, milk, oil, fruit and blend well. Stir together the soda, salt, sugar, flour and then stir into bran mixture.

You can make muffins now, or refrigerate the batter tightly covered for as long as 6 weeks. Stir batter to distribute fruit before using.

*Soak raisins 1 hour in ½ cup boiling water. Drain and add.

Bake in paperlined or greased and floured muffin tins at 375°, 20-25 minutes.

Strawberry Butter

Try this butter recipe for a special occasion.

¾   cup frozen strawberries, drained
1   cup soft butter
3   tablespoons powdered sugar

In a small bowl mix strawberries, butter and sugar well. Serve with muffins, fruit bread or rolls. Makes 1½ cups.

Brunch Menu II

Easier
Curried Fruit
Quick Quiche
Blueberry Cinnamon Muffins

Curried Fruit

The exotic flavor of curry so enhances humble canned fruit that the result is a fancy-tasting dish.

1   29-ounce can peach halves
1   29-ounce can pear halves
1   16½-ounce can pineapple chunks
1   16½-ounce can pitted bing cherries
⅓   cup butter
¾   cup brown sugar
1   teaspoon curry powder

Drain all fruit well and dry on paper towels. Arrange in 1½ quart casserole. Melt butter, add sugar and curry powder, spoon over fruit. Bake 1 hour at 350 degrees. Refrigerate overnight. In the morning allow fruit to come to room temperature, then bake 30 minutes. Allow to stand. Serve warm. Serves 8.

Quick Quiche

This one goes together in minutes, then makes it's own crust while baking.

½ cup biscuit mix
3   eggs
½ cup butter, melted
1½ cups half and half or milk
¼ cup grated Parmesan cheese
1   tablespoon dried minced onion
½ teaspoon dried mustard
1½ cups shredded Swiss or Jack cheese
1   cup diced ham or 8-10 slices bacon, cooked
      and crumbled
¼ teaspoon salt
      dash pepper

In a food processor or blender place biscuit mix, eggs, butter, half and half, Parmesan cheese, onion, mustard, salt and pepper. Mix 30 seconds. Lightly grease a 9" pie plate. Sprinkle cheese and ham on bottom of plate. Pour egg and milk mixture over all. Bake at 350 degrees for 45 minutes.

Blueberry Cinnamon Muffins

These are cake-like muffins brimming with blueberries and topped with brown sugar and a hint of spice.

¼ pound (1 stick) butter
1   cup sugar
2   egg yolks
⅓ cup sour cream or plain yogurt
1½ cups sifted flour
1½ teaspoons baking powder
½ teaspoon cinnamon
½ teaspoon nutmeg
      flour
1   pint fresh or 2 cups frozen blueberries
2   egg whites, stiffly beaten
      brown sugar

In a medium mixing bowl, cream butter and sugar well. Add egg yolks and sour cream and mix again. Sift flour, baking soda, cinnamon and nutmeg. Add to creamed mixture.

Wash, drain and flour blueberries. Fold into batter, Gently fold egg whites into batter and spoon into cupcake paper lined muffin tins or well-greased and floured tins. Sprinkle brown sugar over each muffin. Bake at 375 degrees for 20-25 minutes. Makes about 16 muffins.

Brunch Menu III
Easiest
Fresh Fruit Plate
with Hawaiian Bananas
Sausage Puff
Muffins

PARTY POINTER
- When melons are in season make your own melon balls. Flash freeze on a cookie sheet and store in freezer bags.

Fresh Fruit Plate

Let the season guide you on ingredients for a fruit plate. Fresh melons are wonderful and affordable in season but replac them with frozen melon balls or other fruits when winter arrives. Bananas are consistently reasonable in price. These Hawaiian bananas add a special touch, and of course are do-ahead.

Hawaiian Bananas

- 4 bananas, cut into 6 pieces each
- 1 cup sour cream
- 1 cup flaked coconut
- 2 tablespoons powdered sugar

In a small bowl mix sour cream and powdered sugar. Toast coconut in 350 degree oven until golden. Dip each piece of banana first into sour cream and then into flaked coconut. Place in single layer on plate or pan and refrigerate up to 24 hours. Orange slices and Hawaiian bananas alone also make an attractive fruit salad.

Sausage Puff

- 6 English muffin halves
- 4 eggs
- 2 cups milk
  dash of salt and pepper
- 12 link or brown and serve sausages
- ½ pound Cheddar cheese, shredded

Beat eggs with milk, salt and pepper. In the bottom of a 9" x 9" baking pan arrange and cut muffins to fit. Lightly brown sausages but do not overcook. Arrange sausages on top of muffins. Pour milk and egg mixture over. Sprinkle with cheese. Refrigerate 8 hours or overnight. Then bake at 325 degrees, 45 minutes. Serves 6.

Brunch Menu IV
Simply Elegant
Champagne
Fruit Compote
Curried Ham and Chicken Crepes
Kringla

Fruit Compote
A delightful, do-ahead addition to brunch. This recipe is easy to double or triple for larger groups.

2   tablespoons quick cooking tapioca
2   tablespoons sugar
     dash salt
1½ cups water
1   6-ounce can frozen orange juice
       partially thawed
1   20-ounce can pineapple chunks and juice
½   pint whole strawberries (fresh or frozen)
1   large firm ripe banana

Combine tapioca, sugar, salt and water in saucepan. Stirring constantly, bring to full bubbling boil. Stir this into orange juice in medium bowl. Stir in pineapple and juice. Chill at least 4 hours (or overnight). Just before serving, put in strawberries and banana. Serve in stemmed glasses. Makes 4 servings. Vary fruits as desired: apricots, peaches, cherries, etc.

• Add 1 tablespoon apricot liqueur for a special taste.

Curried Ham and Chicken Crepes

An unusual combination of flavors and textures in a creamy sauce, wrapped in crepes you've made ahead and frozen.

Crepe Recipe

Crepes can be made a month ahead. Cool and stack between layers of waxed paper. Wrap well, label and freeze. Allow to thaw several hours in a refrigerator or 2 hours at room temperature. Crepes must be thawed to roll easily.

- 3 eggs
- ¼ teaspoon salt
- 2 cups all purpose flour
- 2 cups whole milk
- ¼ cup melted butter, margarine or cooking oil

In a medium bowl, combine eggs and salt. Gradually add flour alternately with milk, beating well, using a wire whisk or electric mixer. Beat in melted butter or oil. Cover and refrigerate at least 1 hour or up to 3 days.

Heat a non-stick coated frying pan over medium high heat (or brush a light coat of oil on other type of pan and heat). Place one hand on pan handle and with the other pour 3 tablespoons batter into pan. Immediately lift pan off heat and tilt in all directions so that a thin layer of batter coats the bottom of the pan. Return pan to heat and cook crepe until bottom is browned. Using a spatula carefully turn crepe over. Brown just a minute, then remove crepe to rack to cool. To store, place a piece of waxed paper between each layer of cooled crepes. Slip the stack into a freezer bag and refrigerate up to 5 days or freeze 2 months. Thaw before filling. Makes about 30 8″ crepes.

NOTE: Batter can be made on one day and refrigerated. On another day, make crepes and refrigerate or freeze. Then you can just make filling and sauce, assemble crepes and refrigerate overnight. Bake room temperature crepes covered lightly with foil 20 minutes at 325 degrees. Remove foil and bake 5-10 minutes more. Serve.

Chicken Curry Filling

½ stick butter
1 medium apple, cubed (with skin on)
½ cup celery, chopped
1 small onion, chopped
1 cup mushrooms, fresh or canned
1-2 teaspoons curry
2 cups cooked turkey, cubed, or 1 cup
     turkey and 1 cup ham

Melt butter. Saute vegetables and apple until *just* clear. Then add 2 cups cubed chicken or turkey (ham is also good with either of these). Sprinkle with curry and set all aside. Make white sauce. Add enough white sauce to vegetables and turkey to bind filling together. Place 1 tablespoon filling one each crepe. Roll up tightly and place in a lightly greased 9" x 13" pan. Add ¼ cup of white sauce to bottom of pan before adding crepes. Pour additional sauce over crepes. Makes about 3 cups filling.

White Sauce

Especially easy in the microwave.

5 tablespoons butter
5 tablespoons flour
½ teaspoons salt
2½ cups half and half or cream
2-3 tablespoons white wine

In a small pan melt butter. Stir in flour and cook until bubbly. Remove from heat and add salt, cream and wine, stirring constantly until smooth. Cook over low heat until thick. In a microwave melt butter in microwave safe bowl on high setting. Add flour and salt blending well with wire whisk to form a paste. Gradually add cream and wine, stirring constantly. Microwave on high one minute. Stir. Microwave 1½-2½ minutes longer, stirring every 30 seconds until mixture boils. Stir well. Makes 2½ cups.

Kringla

One friend who doesn't consider herself a good cook, baked this for her father. He wouldn't believe she'd baked it herself and looked for the bakery box.

Crust:
- 1 cup flour
- 2-4 tablespoons water
- ½ cup butter

Puff:
- 1 cup water
- ½ cut butter
- 1 cup flour
- 3 eggs
- ½-1 teaspoon almond extract

Frosting:
- 1 cup powdered sugar
- ½ teaspoon almond extract
- 1 tablespoon butter
- 1-2 tablespoons milk
- ½ cup slivered almonds

Crust and Puff:

In a small bowl mix flour, butter and water to form a dough. Press onto a cookie sheet in two 15" x 3" strips. In a medium saucepan, heat 1 cup water with ½ cup butter to boiling. Remove from heat and add 1 cup of flour. Beat until smooth. Add eggs one at a time, beating hard after each addition. Add almond extract. Spread mixture on crust making sure to seal all the edges. Bake at 375 degrees for 45 minutes. Frost while warm.

Frosting:

Mix powdered sugar, almond extract and butter, mixing well. Add milk a little at a time until glaze is spreading consistency. Sprinkle with almonds.

Cut into strips to serve. Best served the same day.

Luncheon

Luncheons

A luncheon can be a delightful way to entertain. Card parties, showers, birthdays are all perfect luncheon themes. Keep the preparation simple and you'll enjoy a pleasant mid-day gathering.

Try a "Make-Your-Own" luncheon — a salad buffet is an easy and popular one. Serve a soup on arrival and have a dessert tucked in the freezer. Or try Chicken Delight Salad. It's easy and delicious with fruit, muffins and pie for dessert.

MENU

Cream of Tomato Party Soup
Fresh Fruit Kabobs
Chicken Delight Salad
Blueberry Muffins, page 71, 72
Mile High Strawberry Pie, page 49

PARTY POINTERS
- Prepare soup a day ahead and refrigerate. Mix with broth and heat when ready to serve.
- For salad, cube chicken, chop green onions and water chestnuts a day ahead. Place in plastic bags and assemble just before serving.

Cream of Tomato Party Soup

A creamy herb soup that is festive served in small glass cups.

¼ cup fresh dill sprigs or 2 tablespoons
   dried dill
¾ medium onions, sliced
2 10¾-ounce cans cream of tomato soup
1 cup sour cream
¼ teaspoon allspice
   dash pepper
½ teaspoon sugar
2 teaspoons lemon juice
1 cup chicken broth
   chopped parsley or dried parsley

In a processor or blender place dill, onions, soup, sour cream, allspice, pepper, sugar and lemon juice. Process until smooth and creamy. Put in saucepan and stir in chicken broth. Simmer. Sprinkle with parsley. Serves 4-6.

Chicken Delight Salad

A delectable combination of flavors and textures. Great for a large group because it is easy to increase recipe.

2 cups boned chicken, cubed
1 10-ounce package frozen petite French peas
1 cup almonds, slivered
½ cup green onions, chopped
1 can water chestnuts
¾ to 1 cup Best Foods mayonnaise
   leaf lettuce
3 cups chow mein noodles
½ cup almonds, slivered (for garnish)

Combine chicken, raw peas, green onions, water chestnuts, almonds and noodles. Add enough mayonnaise to bind all ingredients together. (Do not add mayonnaise until just before serving or noodles will become soft.) Serve on bed of lettuce. Sprinkle with remaining almonds. Serves 4-6.

Fresh Fruit Kabobs

    wooden skewers
    fresh fruit in season; melons, pineapple, strawberries
    leaf lettuce

Cut wooden skewers into 4" - 6" pieces. Cut fruit into 1" cubes. Leave strawberries whole. Thread fruit onto skewers, alternating colors. For buffet service cover a large glass plate or platter with washed leaf lettuce forming a wheel design. Arrange skewers in spoke fashion over lettuce. Guests take one or several skewers.

For a sit-down luncheon arrange lettuce on plates. Place serving of chicken salad to one side and arrange several kabobs on the other side.

Blueberry Muffins, page 71, 72
    or
Six Week Bran Muffins, page 69

Mile High Strawberry Pie, page 49
    or
Grasshopper Pie, page 86,87
    or
German Sweet Chocolate Pie, page 64

Easy Dinners

Easy Dinner Parties

Nice and Easy Dinner Parties

"We haven't seen the Browns for ages. Let's invite them to dinner." It sounds like fun but sometimes we put off invitations because we think a dinner has to be involved and time consuming. Here are three fuss-free menus. One is an easy one-dish Beef Burgundy. The second is even faster, with chicken as the main dish. The last goes together in just minutes for those occasions when time is at a premium.

EASY DINNER PARTY MENU I
Easy
Brie Almond Melt/Crackers
Tossed Salad
Kathy's Sensational Beef Burgundy
Parmesan Bread Ring
Grasshopper Pie
Coffee

EASY DINNER PARY MENU II
Easier
Pate
Chilled Consomme With Toasted Pita Points
Jane's Chicken Supreme
Suzie's Rice Curry
Gingered Carrots
Dinner Rolls
Cranberry Mousse or
Trifle, page 59

EASY DINNER MENU III
Easiest
Appetizer — Cream Cheese
With Shrimp
Curried Fruit, page 70
Baked Ham Slices
Rice or Baked Potatoes
Suzie's Spinach Side Dish
Frozen Vegetables
Crescent Rolls and Butter
Rich Vanilla Ice Cream
With Liqueur
Crisp Sugar Cookies
Coffee

Easy Dinner Party Menu I
Easy
Brie Almond Melt/Crackers
Tossed Salad
Kathy's Sensational Beef Burgundy
Parmesan Bread Ring
Grasshopper Pie
Coffee

Brie Almond Melt

    1   ounce Brie cheese
    ½   cup almonds, toasted
        Crackers

For conventional oven, place cheese on heatproof dish. Bake in 325 degree oven for 5-8 minutes or until top of cheese begins to sag. Remove from oven and cut halfway around outer edge of cheese and fold this cut piece back. Press almonds into melted top of cheese. Surround with crackers and serve immediately. Guests use crackers to dip out cheese and almonds. A small cluster of grapes makes an attractive garnish.

• Microwave: place cheese on glass plate and microwave 30 seconds. Check to see if soft by pressing down on top of cheese. Microwave additional 10 seconds or press in almonds and serve.

Kathy's Sensational Beef Burgundy

This is a dish men really love. It's filled with meat, carrots, potatoes and onions that are drenched in an incredibly flavorful sauce. It takes about ten minutes to put together and cooks 4-6

85

hours while you're doing something else. It's so good and so easy you'll want to use it as a family meal, too. You might want to mix everything except the potatoes the night before, then just bake the next day.

1½ pounds lean beef stew meat
4   medium size carrots, cut into 2" chunks
4   medium size potatoes, cut into 6 pieces
4   medium size onions, quartered
8   ounces fresh whole mushrooms
2   cans tomato soup
2   1½-ounce packages onion soup mix
1   cup dry red wine
2   tablespoons cornstarch
½   cup cold water

In a 9" x 13" pan place raw stew meat, and add cut carrots, potatoes and onions. If using small mushrooms add them whole or cut large ones in half. In a small bowl mix tomato soup, dry onion mix and wine. Pour mixture over meat and vegetables. Cover all tightly with foil and bake at 325 degrees for 4-6 hours. Mix cornstarch with water and into pan juices to thicken. Serves 4-6.

Parmesan Bread Ring
See page 41

Grasshopper Pie
This rich creamy dessert always gets rave reviews.
Crust:
¼   cup butter, melted
24 Oreos, crushed

In a small bowl, mix butter and crushed Oreos. Press into 9" pie plate. Or use purchased chocolate crumb crust.

Filling:
- 1 7-ounce jar marshmallow creme
- ¼ cup Creme de Menthe
- 2 tablespoons white Creme de Cacao
- 2 cups (one pint) heavy cream, whipped

Place jar of marshmallow creme in bowl of hot water to soften it and make it easier to get out of the jar.

Meanwhile, whip cream in a chilled bowl until very stiff.

Spoon marshmallow creme into blender or processor. Add liqueurs and whip until well blended. Fold carefully into whipped cream. Pour into pie shell and freeze. When firm, cover well. Remove from freezer 15 minutes before serving. Add dollops of whipped cream and shaved chocolate if desired. Serves 6-8.

NOTE: The purchased chocolate crumb crusts are very good and will save you time if needed.

Easy Dinner Party Menu II
Easier
Pate
Chilled Consomme With Toasted Pita Points
Jane's Chicken Supreme
Suzie's Rice Curry
Gingered Carrots
Dinner Rolls
Cranberry Mousse or
Trifle, page 59

Chilled Consommé

Easy and elegant anytime of year, but especially nice in summer.

2 cans Campbell's consommé, chilled
1 lemon cut in pinwheels or wedges

Spoon cold consomme into 8 small, stemmed sherbet glasses. Place a wedge or pinwheel of lemon to the side of consomme glass. Guests can squeeze lemon over consomme and enjoy. Serves 8.

Toasted Pita Points

Serve hot in a napkin-lined basket.

6 pita rounds
1 stick (¼ cup) butter

Separate each pita round into 2 halves. Butter inside of each. Cut each round into 8-10 triangles. Place on a cookie sheet in 400 degree oven. Toast 5 minutes or until golden. Makes 48-60.

Chicken Supreme

Moist chicken in a velvety sauce brimming with mushrooms.

8 large pieces chicken, breasts or thighs
1 can golden mushroom soup
1 cup sour cream
1 cup dry white wine
6 ounces fresh mushrooms or 1-ounce can
     mushrooms, drained
   paprika

In a medium size bowl mix soup, sour cream and wine. Place chicken in 9" x 13" baking pan. Add mushrooms and pour sauce over all. Sprinkle with paprika. Bake uncovered in 325 degree oven for 1½ hours. Serves 8.

Suzie's Rice Curry

Fluffy rice flecked with fruit and nuts.

1   cup raw long grain rice
1   tablespoon instant minced onion
2   teaspoons curry powder
2   beef bouillon cubes
½   teaspoon salt
¼   cup mixed dried fruit, finely chopped
2   tablespoons golden raisins
¼   cup almonds, slivered
2½ cups water
1   tablespoon butter

Mix onion, curry, bouillon, salt, fruit, raisins, almonds, water and butter. Bring water to boil. Add rice. Cover; simmer over low heat 20 minutes. Fluff and serve. Makes 2½ cups. To serve 8 guests, make 2 batches of rice.

Variation:

Instead of rice, serve buttered egg noodles. Sprinkle with chopped or dried minced parsley. To save last minute fuss, cook noodles until almost done. Rinse and cover with water and refrigerate up to 24 hours. When ready to serve, pour noodles into a strainer and dip strainer and noodles into boiling water for 1 minute. Stir noodles around to be sure they are hot. Drain and toss with butter. Serve chicken over noodles. Sprinkle with parsley.

Gingered Carrots

These carrots get a dressed up flavor from a sprinkling of ginger.

4-5 medium carrots, cut in 2″ pieces
½   cup water
2   tablespoons butter
2   tablespoons brown sugar
½   orange, juiced, or 2 tablespoons orange
     juice concentrate
     dash of ginger

In a covered saucepan, simmer carrots until tender. Remove carrots to bowl. Boil remaining carrot water. Add butter, brown sugar and orange juice. Sprinkle in powdered ginger. Return carrots to pan. Cover with sauce. Serve hot.

Variation:

Serve frozen petite peas with butter, in place of carrots. Or try green beans sprinkled with almonds.

Cranberry Mousse

   1 cup cranberry juice cocktail or raspberry-cranberry juice cocktail
   1 3-ounce package raspberry gelatin
   1 16-ounce can jellied cranberry sauce
   1 cup whipping cream, whipped
   (½ cup whipped cream reserved for garnish)

In a medium saucepan heat juice to boiling. Stir in raspberry gelatin until dissolved. Stir in cranberry sauce. Chill until mixture thickens, about an hour. Carefully fold whipped cream into thickened juice mixture. Pour into stemmed glasses or small bowls. Chill several hours or until firm. Garnish with remaining whipped cream.

Easy Dinner Menu III
Easiest

Your spouse has called to say he's bringing the boss and an important client home to dinner. Or an old friend is in town and can only come to dinner tonight. It's 3:00 p.m. and you're working. You don't get off until 5:00 and they'll arrive at 7:00. What can you fix that is special but goes together in minutes? Here's the menu for you. You'll even have time to put your feet up before guests arrive.

Appetizer — Cream Cheese
With Shrimp
Curried Fruit, page 70
Baked Ham Slices
Rice or Baked Potatoes
Suzie's Spinach Side Dish
Frozen Vegetables
Crescent Rolls and Butter
Rich Vanilla Ice Cream
With Liqueur
Crisp Sugar Cookies
Coffee

Cream Cheese with Shrimp

See page 108

Baked Ham Slices

1-2 pounds of ham, sliced 1″ thick
½   cup pineapple juice
1   tablespoon prepared mustard
½   cup brown sugar
½   crushed pineapple

Cut fat around ham in several places to prevent it from curling. Place ham in 3 quart casserole. Add pineapple syrup or juice. Bake covered in 350 degree oven for 40 minutes. Remove from oven; spread with mustard and brown sugar. Spread pineapple over. Bake uncovered 35 minutes. Baste with juice. Serves 6.

Baked Potatoes

Put potatoes in oven 20 minutes before ham. Continue baking with ham. Serve with sour cream and chives.

Suzie's Spinach Side Dish

A creamy flavorful addition to dinner.

3   10-ounce packages frozen chopped spinach, thawed
1   1½-ounce envelope dry onion soup mix
½   pint (1 cup) sour cream
1   2.8 ounce can onion rings

Place thawed spinach in a colander over a bowl. Press down on spinach with a saucer or plate until all water is removed. In a 1½ quart buttered casserole, mix spinach, dry soup mix and sour cream. Bake at 325 degrees for 30 minutes. Sprinkle canned onions over top. Bake 5 minutes and serve. Serves 8.

Dessert

Pretty and quick to fix.

ice cream
liqueurs
cookies

Place ice cream in stemmed glass. Pour liqueur over ice cream and serve on a doily-covered plate with several cookies.

Variations:

- Layer ice cream and liqueur in parfait glasses. Push a pirouette cookie into each side of ice cream.
- Layer mocha ice cream in stemmed glass with crushed chocolate cookies. Sprinkle some reserved crumbs on top.
- For other easy ideas, see Dessert Party, page 58-64.

Tail Gate Party

Tail Gate Party

Calling all sports fans! The excitement of a game just adds to the fun of this picnic, packed at home and served from the back of a station wagon or on a portable table. This is becoming such a popular party that stadium parking lots are often filled with tailgate parties. Adapt the menu to the season and enjoy a moveable feast.

MENU

Sporty Fruit Warm-Up
Oriental Salad
Sweet and Sour Beans
Hot Dogs and Buns
Triple Fudge Pan-Brownies

PARTY POINTERS

- The Spud Party, page 43-46, would make a great tailgate picnic. For this you'll want to wrap the potatoes in foil right out of the oven, using oven mitts. They will stay hot for an hour or more.

- Pack the Sweet and Sour Beans in a crock pot or covered casserole.

- To keep hot dishes hot, first wrap in foil and then in 4 layers of newspaper. Tape closed. This will insulate them for several hours.

- To keep hot dogs hot, place them in a wide mouth

thermos. Fill thermos with boiling water. Hot dogs will heat on the way to the picnic, and the water will keep them hot until serving time.

Sporty Fruit Warm-Up

This warm fruit-and-spice combination is sure to take off the chill at any game. Add a shot of rum or whiskey to each serving, if you're so inclined — a real warm up!

1   6-ounce can orange juice concentrate
1   6-ounce can apple juice concentrate
1   6 ounce can cranberry concentrate
3   sticks cinnamon
8-10 cloves
2   28-ounce bottles 7-Up

In a large saucepan combine orange, apple and cranberry juice concentrates, spices and 7-Up. Simmer 5 minutes. Remove spices. Keep warm in thermos. Makes twelve 6-ounce servings.

NOTE: Place spices in a tea ball for easy removal.

Oriental Salad

This is an excellent "keeper," great for any picnic. Keep it in mind for the next potluck, too, or for a luncheon dish.

½   head (medium-sized) cabbage, shredded*
½   head lettuce, shredded*
4-5 green onions
1   can water chestnuts, sliced
1   cup almonds, slivered and toasted
3   tablespoons sesame seeds, toasted
2   packages of Ramen noodles, crumbled

You could also add mushrooms and/or olives for variation.
*You may use all lettuce or all cabbage. Cabbage will hold up longer.

Toss above ingredients with the following dressing:

Dressing

    1   cup oil
    6   tablespoons vinegar
    4   tablespoons sugar
    1   teaspoon salt
    1½   teaspoons Accent
    ½   teaspoon pepper
    1   packet of noodle seasoning

To use as a main dish or luncheon salad, add 1-2 cups diced chicken or shrimp. Serve with Pita Points, page 88.

Sweet and Sour Beans

Serve these over hot dogs in bun. Recipe on page 16, Sweet and Sour Beans.

Triple Fudge Pan-Brownies

This is a cake you mix, bake and take all in the same pan. It is so fudgy-chocolate in flavor, it is sure to please any chocolate lover on your picnic.

    1   package chocolate fudge cake mix
    1   3½-ounce package instant pudding
    3   eggs, slightly beaten
    ⅓   cup vegetable oil
    1¼   cups water
    1   6-ounce package chocolate chips

Pour cake mix into 9" x 13" baking pan. Mix in instant pudding. Add eggs, stirring with a fork. Stir in oil and water. Be sure to mix batter in the corners of the pan. Stir in chocolate chips. Bake in a 350 degree oven (325 degrees if using a glass pan) for 30-40 minutes.

Theme Parties

Academy Awards Party

Capture all the excitement and glitter of the Academy Awards with your own show stopping party for movie loving friends. The year's nominee movies and stars should give you plenty of ideas. Here are some general star suggestions:

PARTY POINTERS

- Invitations could look like movie tickets.

- Cut out pictures of nominees from movie magazines. Make a collage to greet guests at the front door.

- Cut stars out of silver paper or use jumbo star stickers. Glue a picture of nominee in center of each one. Tape to wooden skewers and push into flower arrangement.

- Sprinkle glitter on tablecloth or buffet table for a shimmering effect.

- Serve popcorn in small paper bags like a movie theater.

- Ask guests to come dressed as a favorite nominee or character played.

- Cut out stars and use clear plastic thread or fishing line to hang them from light fixture over buffet table.

- Arrange to play the nominated music or themes from nominated movies.

- Give guests ballots on arrival and let them cast their votes.

- Have movie tickets as prizes if guests come in costume.

- Depending on the zaniness of the group, guests who are dressed as nominees could make their own acceptance speeches.

MENU IDEAS

The current list of nominees will give you ideas for other names for dishes. Use names of stars or movies and look for special items that might suggest a certain movie, Reese's Pieces from the movie E.T. or indian rice or curry for the movie Ghandi. Once you get started, similar ideas will come to you.

Here are some other general ideas for food and names:

Ham
Champagne or Sparkling Cider
"Say Cheese" Cheese Ball
Hollywood Cheesecake
"14 Carrots"
Picture Perfect Pork
Starlet Punch
Premiere Potatoes
Opening Night Vegetables
Star-Struck Stroganoff
Million Dollar Dessert

Kentucky Derby Party

Friends who enjoy a good horse race love this Kentucky Derby Party. You'll all gather 'round the T.V. to follow the race and then enjoy a buffet that will always come in first, in Southern style.

MENU
Mock Mint Juleps
Plantation Chowder
Southern Fried Chicken
Refrigerator Mashed Potatoes
Colonel's Carrots
Buttermilk Biscuits/Honey Butter
Pecan Pie

PARTY POINTERS
- Sugar syrup for juleps can be done ahead.
- Chowder can be made ahead and reheated. Add parsley and chopped onions just before serving.
- Sweet Potato Casserole can be done up to 2 days ahead.
- Refrigerator Mashed Potatoes can be done up to 2 weeks ahead.
- Pecan Pie is best done early the day of the party but can be done a day ahead.

Mock Mint Juleps

A real Mint Julep takes careful preparation and is made individually. This quick version is an easier way to toast the winning horse. Fresh mint is an absolute must.

1½ cups sugar
2 cups water
   juice of 3 lemons
8 springs of mint, bruised to release flavor
1 quart gingerale
   Kentucky bourbon
   crushed ice
   powdered sugar

In a medium to large saucepan boil sugar and water. Cool. Add lemon juice, mint and gingerale. Fill 8 glasses half full of crushed ice. Pour 1 to 2 ounces bourbon over ice. Fill with drink mixture and garnish with a sprig of mint. Use a small sifter to sprinkle powdered sugar over top.

NOTE: Prepare water and sugar syrup ahead of time and simply add other ingredients.

Plantation Chowder

A hearty but quick first course.

2 10¾-ounce cans condensed cream of potato soup
1 pint half and half or heavy cream
½ cup milk
2 17-ounce cans whole kernel corn or 1 can
   creamed and one whole kernel
2 tablespoons butter or margarine
8 ounces sausage, cooked and crumbled or 10
   slices bacon, cooked and crumbled
1 tablespoon minced fresh parsley or 1
   teaspoon dried
4-6 green onions, finely chopped

In a large saucepan heat soup with half and half and milk until hot, stirring often. Add corn, butter and sausage.

101

Sprinkle with minced parsley and green onions. Makes 8 servings.

Variation:

• Use one cup finely chopped cooked ham in place of sausage or bacon.

• Brown and serve sausage will give you another head start.

Southern Fried Chicken

Use your own favorite recipe and keep warm in the oven. Garnish platter with parsley before serving.

Refrigerator Mashed Potatoes

What a time saver! This do ahead dish will keep up to two weeks in the refrigerator and tastes fantastic. Adapt it for large groups and for a great Thanksgiving do ahead.

8-9 large potatoes, about 5 pounds
2   3-ounce packages cream cheese
1   cup dairy sour cream
2   teaspoons onion powder
1   teaspoon salt
    dash of pepper
    dash or nutmeg
3   tablespoons butter or margarine
1   cup grated Cheddar cheese (optional)

Cook potatoes in salted water until done. Drain. Mash until smooth with masher or mixer. Add cream cheese, sour cream, onion powder, salt, pepper, nutmeg and butter. Place in suitable refrigerator container. Allow to cool. To heat, place potatoes in a casserole dish and bake at 350°, 20-30 minutes. Sprinkle with cheese last 5 minutes. Makes 8 cups of potatoes.

Fresh or Frozen Green Peas

Steamed or cooked according to package directions.

The Colonel's Carrots

See Ginger Carrots, page 89-90.

Buttermilk Biscuits

A biscuit mix makes these quick to fix or buy the refrigerator variety. You simply bake and serve.

Honey Butter

A melt in your mouth companion to biscuits.

½ cup (1 stick) butter
3 tablespoons honey

In a small bowl mix butter and honey well. Serve with biscuits.

Pecan Pie

A sumptuous southern classic.

3 eggs, beaten
1 cup dark corn syrup
1 cup dark brown sugar, packed
1 tablespoons butter, melted
   dash of salt
1 teaspoon vanilla extract

1 9" pie shell, unbaked

1 cup pecan halves, cut in half
1 cup sweetened whipped cream and chopped pecans
   for garnish (optional)

In a medium bowl, mix eggs, corn syrup, brown sugar, butter and salt. Pour into unbaked pie shell. Sprinkle nuts over filling. Bake at 375 degrees, 40-45 minutes.

NOTE: Pillsbury's refrigerated pie dough is very good. Try it if time is short.

Cocktail Party/
Open House

Cocktail Party/Open House

A Cocktail Party or Open House can be easy on the host and hostess, because much of the preparation is done well in advance, leaving everyone free to enjoy the party. The menu should be varied, and this list of recipes fits that bill — plus each is "do-ahead," or can be put together in less than five minutes.

PARTY POINTERS
- When planning the menu, keep in mind that you'll want a variety of colors in the food.
- Add parsley, cherry tomatoes, carrot flowers (see garnishes, page 115, to dress up less colorful dishes).
- Keep texture in mind, too. Serve the Mini Quiche or Cream Puffs, but include another item with crisp crackers, and a platter of crunchy fresh vegetables with dips.
- Select variety in flavors. Even though you may adore spicy food, some people prefer a milder fare. Serve the Mexican Nacho dish, but provide a less spicy cheesball and round crackers, too.
- Most people are standing at a cocktail party, so keep this in mind when planning decorations. Place some high, so they'll be seen.
- If your party is a large one, plan for extra refrigerator space, perhaps at a neighbor's.
- Finally, you'll want to serve some hot items as well as some cold. Select recipes that taste good once they've cooled down a bit, too.

Parmesan Puffs

The mixture for this delicious treat will keep beautifully for weeks, ready to serve guests at a moment's notice.

1 cup real mayonnaise
1 tablespoon onion, minced
⅓ cup Parmesan cheese, grated
2 tablespoons Sherry or white wine
    Ritz crackers

Mix all ingredients except crackers. Place mixture in a covered container in the refrigerator. To serve, place a teaspoon of the mixture on a Ritz cracker. Place on cookie sheet and broil just until golden, about 1 minute (watch them carefully). Serve immediately. Makes about 40 snacks.

Marvelous Mousse

If you're splurging add the crab. Otherwise, this is excellent with just the vegetables. The cucumber gives it a nice fresh taste.

1 can cream of mushroom soup
1 envelope unflavored gelatin
1 8-ounce package cream cheese, cut into cubes
½ cup mayonnaise
½ cup sour cream
1 cup celery, finely chopped
1 bunch green onions, chopped, greens and all
6 ounces of crabmeat or 1 large cucumber, peeled
    and chopped

In a medium saucepan, place soup. Sprinkle with gelatin and heat to boiling, stirring constantly. Remove from heat and stir in cubes of cream cheese. Stir until melted. Blend in mayonnaise and sour cream. Add celery, onions and crabmeat or cucumber. Pour into lightly greased 1 quart mold and refrigerate several hours or up to 2 days. To serve, unmold on large plate. Garnish with parsley and lemon wedges and surround with plain round crackers. Serves 8-10.1

If using crab, use a fish shaped mold. Cut a cucumber into paper thin slices. Cut each slice in half and arrange as scales on the fish. Use slices of olive for eyes.

Brown's Bottom Clams

The chiles give this a south-of-the-border flavor.

1   7-ounce can clams
1   3-ounce package cream cheese
     dash Worcestershire sauce
¼   teaspoon curry powder
1   teaspoon dry chopped onion
¼   teaspoon garlic powder
2   tablespoons (or to taste) chopped
        green chiles
½   pound Cheddar cheese, shredded
6   English muffins

Mix and refrigerate overnight. Pile on 10-12 English muffin halves. Broil until bubbly — 3-5 minutes. Cut each muffin into 4 or more pieces. Makes 40-60 pieces.

Strawberry Supreme

When fruit is in season this is a colorful complement to any cocktail menu.

1   quart strawberries
1   pint sour cream
¾   cup brown sugar

Place rinsed and dried strawberries in a bowl or napkin lined basket. Place sour cream and brown sugar in 2 separate bowls. Guests dip strawberries first in cream, then in sugar, and eat.

Artichoke Heaven

1   14-ounce can artichoke hearts, drained and cut up
1½ cups mayonnaise
1½ cups Parmesan cheese
2   cloves garlic, crushed

In small bowl mix artichokes, mayonnaise, cheese and garlic. Pour into small casserole or souffle dish and bake at 325 degrees until puffed and golden. Do not overbake or it will separate. Can be done in a microwave oven. Serve hot with crackers.

Brie Almond Melt

See recipe, page 85.

Instant Cream Cheese Logs

With cream cheese on hand, you can whip up an hors d'oeuvre that's fast and flavorful in minutes.

Place an 8-ounce package of cream cheese on a glass plate. Then: pour ¼ cup seafood sauce over cheese. Cover sauce with ½-1 cup small shrimp and sprinkle with fresh minced parsley. Or . . . pour ½ cup of chutney over the cheese block. Or . . . pour about a cup of jalapeno jelly over the cheese block. Or . . . pour 1 cup green mint jelly over the cheese block. Serve any of these with an assortment of crackers.

Quick Mini Quiche

A mini mouthful of sausage and cheese. Double or triple recipe for a party of more than 8 guests.

36 wonton skins
3   eggs
¾   cup heavy cream or half and half
3   tablespoons dried minced onion flakes
½   pound sausage, cooked and drained
1½ cups shredded jack cheese (or you can
      use Cheddar, or even a mixture of cheeses)
      dried parsley flakes
      mini-cupcake pans
      biscuit cutter
      Pam spray

In a medium frying pan saute sausage. Drain and set aside. In a small bowl beat eggs and cream. Use a biscuit cutter to cut wonton skins to fit your mini pans. Spray pans with Pam. Press cut wontons into pans. Sprinkle some sausage and cheese into the bottom of each wonton shell. Sprinkle a few dried minced onions over sausage and cheese. Pour egg and cream mixture over all, filling just to the top. Sprinkle some dried parsley flakes on top. Bake in a 325 degree oven for 15-20 minutes. Mini Quiche are done done when knife inserted in center comes out clean. Makes 36 Mini Quiche.

To freeze, remove from mini pans and place on a rack to cool. Place on a cookie sheet and flash freeze. When frozen, about 30 minutes, lay quiche in freezer bags and stack in freezer. To serve, heat frozen quiche 5-8 minutes in 325 degree oven and serve hot, warm or room temperature.

Variations:

- For bacon quiche, use ½ pound crumbled bacon in place of sausage.

- For spinach quiche, use 1 package of thawed Stouffer's spinach souffle in place of egg mixture. Use with or without sausage, cheese and onion.

Sausage Balls

1 pound package bulk sausage, mild or hot
1½ cups baking mix
3 cups grated sharp Cheddar cheese

In a medium bowl, mix room temperature sausage, biscuit mix, and cheese, using hands to knead until ingredients are blended. Shape into 1" balls. Place on an ungreased cookie sheet and bake at 400 degrees for 12-14 minutes. Makes about 60 balls. Recipe can be easily multiplied for large groups.

- Do-ahead tip: Sausage balls can be frozen unbaked. Flash freeze on a cookie sheet. When frozen place in freezer bags. Bake frozen balls 18-20 minutes. Serve hot.

Variation:
Serve with a sweet and sour sauce as a dip.

Cheeseball

1 8-ounce package cream cheese
3 jars processed cheese spread: Bacon, Sharp Cheddar, or Old English
¾ cup chopped nuts
chopped parsley (optional)
several nut halves (optional)

Mix room temperature cream cheese and cheese spread in a food processor or with an electric mixer. Refrigerate mixture about one hour for easy rolling. Roll cheese into one or two large balls, or 1" balls for individual servings. Spread chopped nuts on a plate and roll cheeseball until covered. Press a nut half into center of each ball. Wrap well in plastic wrap and refrigerate for up to 2 weeks, or wrap in foil and freeze for 4-6 weeks. Thaw in refrigerator 6 hours or at room temperature 1 hour. Serve at room temperature with crackers.

NOTE: If using food processor do not overprocess.

Lindsey's Minute Pate

A glamorous first course that's party perfect.

8   ounces bratwurst, at room temperature
8   ounces cream cheese, softened
¼   cup onion, very finely minced
1   clove garlic, minced or crushed
    dash of Worcestershire sauce
    dash of salt and pepper
    chopped parsley

In a medium size bowl, mix the bratwurst, cream cheese, onion, garlic, Worcestershire sauce, salt and pepper. Form into a ball or log. Roll in parsley. Or place mixture in a crock and top with parsley. Serve with crackers or toast points. Makes 1 cup.

Nacho Plate

A pretty dish men really like. Barbara Hoffa shared her recipe with me.

1   pound lean ground beef
1   large onion, chopped
1-2 cans (1 pound each) refried beans
2-3 cups jack or mild Cheddar cheese, shredded
     salsa brava (hot sauce) to individual
         taste (optional)

Garnishes: (your choice)

¼   cup green onions, chopped   3   medium tomatoes
1   can black olives, chopped   parsley sprigs
2-3 mashed avocados   lettuce, chopped
1   cup sour cream

Brown ground beef and onion and discard fat. Spread refried beans in 9" x 13" ovenproof pan. Top with ground beef. Add cheese. Drizzle taco and hot sauce on top. (At this point, dish may be refrigerated for up to 24 hours.) Bake uncovered at 400 degrees for 20-25 minutes. Add garnishes and serve with taco chips.

Chicken Wings

Many meat departments carry trimmed chicken wings in small packages and at special savings in 5 pound bags. Ask your meat man if you can't find them.

40 trimmed chicken wings
1 18-ounce bottle Kraft Hickory Smoke
   Barbeque Sauce

In a 9" x 13" pan, arrange chicken wings. Pour enough barbeque sauce over to cover wings. Bake uncovered for 1½ hours at 325 degrees.

- Wings can be cooked, flash frozen and put in freezer bags. To serve arrange on a cookie sheet and heat about 8 minutes at 325 degrees.

- For shorter storage, prepare wings, bake, cool and refrigerate covered for 2-3 days. Reheat for 5 minutes at 325 degrees.

- To serve, arrange pinwheel fashion on a round plate. Arrange a large bunch of parsley in the center with several cherry tomatoes.

Stuffed Mushrooms

Creamy and tangy.

1   8-ounce package cream cheese
1   teaspoon milk
1   envelope Good Seasons Italian or Bleu
      Cheese Salad Dressing Mix
5   green onions, chopped
¾   pounnd medium size fresh mushrooms,
      stems removed
     paprika

In a small bowl mix cream cheese, milk, dressing mix, green onions and chopped mushroom stems. Use mixture to stuff mushroom caps. Broil 3-5 minutes – until golden brown. Sprinkle with paprika.

Bacon-Wrapped Breadsticks

Quick and crunchy.

1   pound bacon, thinly sliced
48 3" breadsticks, or longer ones broken in half
      wine mustard or regular prepared mustard

Cut bacon strips in half. Brush breadsticks with mustard. Wrap bacon tightly around breadsticks. Broil on broiler pan until golden brown, about 5 minutes. Makes 48 hors d'oeuvres.

• Prepared breadsticks may be wrapped and refrigerated overnight. Then broiled before serving.

Saucy Dogs

Ready to enjoy in 5 minutes.

1   10-ounce jar current jelly
⅔ l cup prepared mustard
1   pound hot dogs cut into 1"-2" pieces

In medium size saucepan, melt jelly. Stir in mustard. Add hot dog pieces and simmer 3 minutes. Serve from a fondue pot or chafing dish with toothpicks for spearing.

NOTE: Try mixed fruit jelly in place of current jelly for a less expensive treat.

Vegetable Bouquet and Dip (on cover)

Crisp, crunchy vegetables and a creamy dip are a must at any party. This presentation turns a sometimes boring arrangement into a conversation piece. The bouquet looks as if you'd spent hours, but actually it's done very quickly with cookie cutters, a fluted cutter and wooden skewers. Serving the dip in a flower pot is a charming touch.

- 6 turnips – 2 large, 2 medium, 2 small
- 8 medium and large carrots
- 1 bunch green onions
- 1 medium bunch celery
- 1 head cauliflower
- 1 bunch broccoli
- 1 pint cherry tomatoes
- 1 bunch radishes
- 1 large cucumber
- 1 zucchini
- 1 bunch leaf lettuce
- 1 small cabbage to fit into basket

Other additions might include:

giant olives – black and/or green
tiny whole pickles
wooden skewers
flower pot shaped basket or small round dish
bowls of ice water
metal flower cookie cutters

Cut all vegetables ahead of time and refrigerate up to 2 days. To make turnip flowers, cut the turnip into ¼" rounds. Cut flower shapes with cookie cutter. Peel and cut medium carrots – cut into enough ¼" rounds to make centers for each of your flowers. To assemble, place carrot round in center of each turnip flower. Push pointed skewer through both and arrange in "bouquet."

To make onion mums cut the root off of a green onion. Cut off all but 2" of green part, leaving a 3" piece of the white, with some green. Using a very sharp paring knife, cut 1" into the white part. Make 4-5 cuts. Place cut onion into ice water. In several hours it will "bloom" as the cut pieces curl back and form curly petals.

To make carrot flowers cut larger carrots into ½" rounds. With the tip of a sharp knife cut tiny triangles out of carrot rim forming look of petals. To arrange in bouquet, push skewer into center or into edge like a lollipop.

Cut broccoli and cauliflower into flowerettes (the top part of each vegetable). Skewer and add to bouquet.

Remove ½ strips of cucumber skin leaving a striped effect all around the vegetable. Cut into ¼" rounds and push skewer into edge when ready to add to bouquet.

Tomatoes are simply skewered and added to the arrangement. Treat large olives and midget pickles the same way.

To assemble bouquet: Wedge cabbage into basket or other container. (Remove outer leaves if too large, yet fit should be tight.) Cover cabbage with curly lettuce leaves or with parsley, securing with toothpicks.

Push skewered vegetables into cabbage in an attractive arrangement, making them different heights. If using as a centerpiece, remember to make arrangement attractive on all sides. To arrange bouquet hours ahead, sprinkle arrangement lightly with water, cover with plastic wrap and refrigerate.

Keep extra "flowers" in water in refrigerator to replenish bouquet during party.

Bacon Wrap-Ups

Crunchy and delicious.

1   pound bacon, cut into 3"-4" pieces
2   tablespoons mustard
2   can whole water chestnuts
2   tablespoons brown sugar
1   cup teriyaki sauce
    toothpicks

Spread bacon with thin coat of mustard. Sprinkle with a little brown sugar. Wrap each water chestnut with bacon (cut very large water chestnuts in half) and secure with toothpick. Arrange in glass dish and pour teriyaki sauce over all. Marinate several hours or overnight. Place wrap-ups on cookie sheet and broil until golden. Serve hot.

Tomato Bites

A can of deviled ham is a great item to keep on your party shelf.

1   can deviled ham
1   pint cherry tomatoes
    parsley

Cut an "X" in the top of each tomato, cutting halfway through the tomato. Stuff with deviled ham. Top each tomato with a tiny sprig of parsley. This can be done a day ahead, covered and refrigerated. Serve on a bed of lettuce leaves or parsley.

NOTE: To extend the deviled ham you could add one or two chopped hard-cooked eggs. Add mayonnaise to bind together.

Mexicali Mix

Creamy and spicy.

1   15-ounce can chili without beans
1   8-ounce package cream cheese
    Taco Chips

In a small saucepan heat chili and cream cheese until cheese melts, or melt right in glass dish in microwave oven, stirring several times. Serve with Taco Chips. Makes about 2 cups dip.

Kathy's Teriyaki Wings

24   chicken wingettes
½   cup white wine or sherry
½   cup soy sauce
2   tablespoons brown sugar
2-3   cloves garlic, finely minced
4   green onions, finely chopped or 1 tablespoon
      powdered ginger

Cut wings in half at joint. Mix soy sauce, wine, sugar, garlic, onion and ginger. Marinate wings in glass baking pan 2 hours or overnight. Do not drain. Bake in same dish at 350 degrees for 1 hour.

Holiday Faire

Caroling Party

Singing through the neighborhood with my aunts, uncles and cousins is a warm and fond memory for me. We'd all practice 'round the piano first. Then off we'd go to spread our own brand of holiday cheer until our teeth chattered so hard we couldn't sing and we'd have to come in for steaming hot chocolate.

Singing just brings out the joy and holiday spirit in everyone, so invite neighbors and friends to meet at your house or perhaps at your church to carol throughout the neighborhood. If there's a song leader and a guitarist so much the better, but don't worry if your group is without. Assign someone to start the songs and someone to pick the next song and after just a little practice you're off to spread holiday cheer.

The menu can be as simple as hot chocolate and Christmas cookies or a little heartier buffet of soup, crusty bread and bar cookies. Keep in mind the fresh air makes people hungry.

MENU

Percolated Punch
and
Hot Chocolate
Christmas Cookies
or
Vickie's Vegetable Soup
Crusty Bread
Oriental Salad, page 95, 96
or
Layered Salad, page 14
Coconut Bar Cookies, page 129
or
Christmas Cookies/Fruit Breads

119

PARTY POINTERS
- Be sure all the singers have copies of the songs.
- The group could practice a few songs as you wait for all the guests to arrive.
- Serve Percolated Punch and nuts and a snack mix as guests arrive.
- Remind people to dress warmly and to bring flashlights.
- Gather up some extra wool hats, gloves, umbrellas and flashlights.
- Try to stay in a tight group while singing so you'll all stay together musically.

Variations:
- You might choose the Cheese Bread, page 41, or the Parmesan Bread Ring, page 41.
- Your caroling party could even be a do-it-yourself party like The Pizza, Omelette or Stewpendous.

Pecolated Punch

It's steaming, spicy and easy to do in a percolator. You could use a drip coffee maker and pour juice through machine. Follow by running clear water through or it could affect the taste of the next pot of coffee. For a large group make several pots or multiply recipe and use a 35 cup pot.

    2   cups cranberry juice
    2½ cups apple juice or unsweetened
            pineapple juice
    ½   cup water
    ⅓   cup brown sugar
    1½ teaspoons whole cloves
    1½ teaspoons whole allspice
    3   sticks cinnamon, broken into pieces

Place juices and water in a percolator. Place sugar and spices in percolator basket. Percolate 10-12 minutes. Makes 8 servings.

Cookie-Baking Party

Baking cookies is as traditional as the tree is at Christmas. Why not turn the event into a party? Of course children love this idea and it makes a perfect party for them, but don't forget that everyone enjoys cutting out cookies and going creative with decorations, no matter what the age. So this makes a good teen or adult party, too.

You might serve hot chocolate or punch on arrival and then serve soup and a sandwich lunch as the cookies bake.

MENU

Hot Chocolate or Punch
Mugs of Soup and Sandwiches
Cookies

PARTY POINTERS
- Preparation is the key here. Mix up the cookie dough a day or two ahead and refrigerate it. Recipe, page 125.
- Keep extra dough chilled until ready to roll out and cut. It will roll more easily and not take up extra flour which can make cookies tough.
- Arrange rolling and cutting area as follows:
    - Bowl of flour to sprinkle on board before rolling
    - Rolling pins — borrow several so there is no waiting
    - Basket of cutters
    - Flat bowl with flour in it. Instruct bakers to dip cutter into flour and shake off excess. This will prevent dough from sticking to cutters.

- Straws for cutting holes in top of cookies. Make holes big enough to allow for rising when cookies are baked.
  - Cookie sheets
  - Racks for cooling
- Arrange decorating area as follows:
  - Bowls of white and colored frosting
  - Small bowls or shaker bottles of chocolate shot and colored sugars.
  - Tubes of colored frosting to pipe around cookies.
  - Narrow ribbons or yarn in bright colors to pull through holes in cookies so they can be hung from tree.
  - Have some cookies already made for nibbling as guests arrive and as they prepare their cookies.
  - Be sure to provide small boxes so guests can transport cookie creations home safely.
- Giant cookie cutters are popular and would be especially good for this party.

- If you just don't have time to mix your own cookie dough, try a cookie mix or the refrigerator dough in the roll. Children can still have a great time cutting, baking and decorating.

- As extra entertainment as cookies bake, arrange bowls of large marshmallows, raisins, whole cloves and toothpicks. Children can make little snowmen.

Christmas Cookie Exchange

The cookie exchange is a delightful way to have a variety of cookies for your holiday table. The hostess invites her guests. They bring cookies to exchange with other guests. Each guest brings as many cookies as she would like to exchange, plus some for the table. Everyone can relax and visit and then take home a selection of different cookies for holiday entertaining. Even the hostess enjoys this party, because all she has to do is prepare coffee and tea and any cookies she might like to exchange. All the cookies to serve are made for her.

A telephone call could be used to invite each guest or you may wish to send out invitations. Select your own wording or use the poem on the next page for your invitation.

MENU
Coffee
Tea
Christmas Fruit Punch
Cookies, page 125
Nuts
Mints

It's the time of the year
    when best cookies are made
What fun to make extra in order to trade
Please come on — —-(date)— —-
    bringing cookies, your best
Exchange yours for others and so will each guest
Bring as many to trade as you want
    to take home
And some for the table for we're sure
    not to roam
Until we've had coffee, tea and a chat
    and welcomed the season
There's reason for that.
Our baking is done, we'll relax,
    we are free
So sing Merry Christmas from you
    and from me.

PARTY POINTERS

- Guests bring cookies in groups of 6 or 12, arranged so that other guests can take them home.
- Cookies can be arranged on a small paper Christmas plate, covered with plastic wrap and tied with ribbon.
- Or line tiny plastic produce baskets from cherry tomatoes, etc., with a Christmas napkin, fill with cookies, and wrap in plastic and ribbon.
- Even gingham paper lunch sacks could be used for cookies.
- There are also attractive small cartons and carriers available in stationery and paper stores.
- Arrange a table, counter or buffet where everyone places cookies to trade.
- Serve a flavored coffee from a coffee shop as an accompaniment to the cookies.
- Offer decaffeinated coffee, too. It also comes flavored.

Endless Variations of Butter Cookies
Basic Dough

1   cup butter
1½   cups sifted powdered sugar
1   egg
1   teaspoon vanilla
2½   cups flour
1   teaspoon baking soda
1   teaspoon cream of tartar
¼   teaspoon salt

In a large mixing bowl cream butter. Add sugar gradually, cream until fluffy. Add unbeaten egg and vanilla. Beat well. Sift together flour, soda, cream of tartar and salt. Blend into creamed mixture. Divide dough. Prepare variations:

Variations:
Butter Crispies (rolled)

Chill half a recipe of basic dough. Roll on well floured pastry cloth to one-eighth inch thick. Cut with floured cookie cutters. Bake about 6 minutes. Cool on cake racks. Makes about 3 dozen. Decorate as desired.

Snowballs

To half recipe of basic dough add ¾ cup ground walnuts. Chill. Roll dough into balls the size of large marbles. Bake 8 to 10 minutes. Roll at once in powdered sugar. Cool. Roll again in sugar. Makes 2½ dozen.

Butter Fingers

To one half of basic dough recipe add ½ cup chopped nuts and ¼ cup chopped candied cherries. Chill. Shape into oblongs the size of a little finger. Bake 8 to 10 minutes. Sprinkle while hot with granulated sugar and again when cool. Makes 2 dozen.

Trixie Treats

Chill half recipe of basic dough. Mold into balls the size of walnuts. Roll in mixture of 2 tablespoons sugar and 1 teaspoon cinnamon. Bake 8 to 10 minutes. Makes about 2½ dozen.

Butter Thinsies (Refrigerator cookies.)

Roll half of basic dough recipe in a roll 2 inches in diameter. Wrap in waxed paper. Chill until firm. Slice one-eighth inch thick. Sprinkle with finely chopped nuts or coconut. Bake 6 minutes. Makes about 3 dozen.

Chocolate Mint Creams

To half of basic dough add 1 square unsweetened chocolate, melted and cooled. Form dough in roll 2 inches in diameter. Wrap in waxed paper. Chill. Slice one-eighth inch thick. Bake 8 minutes. Cool. Put two together with filling: 2 T. butter, 1 cup sifted powdered sugar, 1 T. cream, mint flavoring to taste and a drop of green food coloring. Makes 30 wafers.

Orange Snow Balls

If time gets away from you before you can bake some cookies for the holidays, whip up these no-bake, melt-in-your-mouth goodies. As their base they have store-bought shortbread cookies. They make 'baking" a breeze. Triple recipe for cookie exchange.

1   package shortbread cookies, crushed
1   cup coconut, flaked
⅔   cup powdered sugar, sifted
½   cup thawed, frozen orange juice concentrate or
      lemonade concentrate for Lemon Snowballs
   sifted powdered sugar for coating

Mix cookie crumbs, coconut and ⅔ cup powdered sugar in medium size bowl. Stir in orange juice concentrate until well blended. Roll mixture a teaspoon at a time into balls. Roll each ball in powdered sugar, coating generously. Place each cookie in a paper candy cup. Makes about 40 cookies.

Tree Cutting Party

Driving out to a tree farm, picking out the perfect tree, and then cutting it down yourself adds a bit of Christmas past to your holiday. Gather a group of friends and family and plan a tree cutting expedition. Once each cutter and his "advisers" have found the perfect tree, serve a Tail Gate Picnic. Everyone will enjoy an alfresco feast. Or serve the picnic at home around a roaring fire.

As a personal note I might add that trees often look much smaller out in the open than they do in your living room. One year we brought home a tree nearly two feet taller than our ceiling. Even after we cut it to fit, the boughs were so wide we had to trim them with hedge shears and move much of the furniture out of the room! But it *was* one of the most beautiful trees ever.

MENU
Hot Spiced Wine
or
Hot Chocolate
Raw Fresh Vegetables
Chili with Toppings
Sour Dough Rolls
Coconut Bar Cookies
Fresh Fruit

PARTY POINTERS
- Use mugs for the chili for easy serving.
- See menu for Tail Gate Party, page 94-96.
- See menu for Spud Party, page 43-46, as a Tail Gate Party.

Hot Spiced Wine

A fruity, full bodied warm up.

1 cup water
1 lemon, sliced
1 stick cinnamon
⅓-½ cup sugar
1 bottle claret or sweet red wine
3 cups orange juice

Boil water with lemon, cinnamon, cloves, and sugar for 5 minutes. Strain and mix with wine and arrange juice. Heat and serve warm.

For Tail Gate Picnic, transport in thermos. Serves 8.

Chili Con Carne

Chili means "meat with peppers" in Spanish. This is a quick version when time is short.

1½ pounds hamburger
2   medium onions, chopped
2   tablespoons vegetable oil
3   cloves garlic, minced
1   teaspoon salt
1-2 teaspoons chili powder
¼   teaspoon pepper
2   cups canned tomatoes, coarsely chopped, undrained.
1   15-ounce can kidney beans, drained.

In a medium frying pan, brown ground beef, onions and garlic in vegetable oil. Add salt, chili, pepper. Add tomatoes and kidney beans and stir well. Simmer over low heat 20-30 minutes. Serves 6.

Variation:

• Use 2 10-ounce cans tomato soup in place of canned tomatoes.

Toppings for Chili

sour cream
Parmesan cheese
corn chips
grated Cheddar cheese
green onions, chopped

Coconut Bar Cookies

These chewy bars go together in just minutes — and all right in the baking pan.

½ cup butter or margarine
2 cups graham cracker crumbs
1 14-ounce can Eagle Brand condensed milk or
       homemade condensed milk, page 19
1 6-ounce package semi-sweet chocolate chips
1 cup coconut
1 cup walnuts, chopped

In a 9″ x 9″ baking pan, melt butter right in preheating oven. Remove pan from oven and spread butter evenly over bottom of pan. Sprinkle graham cracker crumbs over butter. Press down, forming crust. Sprinkle chocolate chips over crumbs. Cover chocolate chips with a layer of condensed milk. Sprinkle with a layer of nuts and then coconut. Return pan to oven and bake at 350 degrees for 15 minutes or until coconut is golden. Cool. Cut into bars.

Tree Decorating Party

As the woodsy scent of a freshly cut tree fills the air, friends gather to deck the tree and share holiday cheer. Add Christmas music in the background and who can resist singing carols as the tree is dressed for the season.

Put out all the ornaments and guests enjoy refreshments that include vegetables served from a tabletop edible "tree" and hot buttered rum or punch. Food could be a more ample lunch or buffet. Try menus from the Ornament Making Party or any of the soup and bread menus.

MENU

Hot Buttered Rum
Punch
Edible Christmas Tree
Cheeseball, page 110
or
Plantation Chowder, page 101
Cheese Bread, page 41
Triple Fudge Brownies, page 96

PARTY POINTERS

- Some popcorn for stringing is fun. Stale popcorn doesn't break as easily as fresh.
- Organize your ornaments and lights for easy access by guests.
- Check for burned out bulbs.
- Buy extra ornament hangers.

An Edible Christmas Tree

This festive centerpiece is part of the refreshments, and is custom made for a tree decorating party. Serve the green dip to accompany the crispy vegetables.

1   head cauliflower
10-15 radishes
1   bunch broccoli
1   bunch celery
3-4 medium carrots
1   bunch green onions
1   jar cocktail onions
1   14-ounce can giant black olives
1   pint cherry tomatoes
3   large bunches parsley
    sharp paring knife
    toothpicks or florist picks
    14″ styrofoam cone

Wash all vegetables. Trim flowerettes from cauliflower and broccoli. Cut radishes to make petals, page 115. Cut celery into 2″ pieces. Cut slits at both ends not quite to center. Place in ice water to curl ends. Cut green onions and trim to make flowers, page 115. Place in ice water to "bloom." Cut carrot flowers, page 115. Place each kind of vegetable in a separate plastic bag and refrigerate until ready to assemble tree. Be sure to have some vegetables in reserve to add to tree as guests enjoy those on tree. Place tree on round platter or tray. Cover entire tree with parsley, holding in place with toothpicks or florist picks.

Skewer vegetables with toothpicks and stick them into tree in an attractive arrangement.

NOTE: Dip — Use a commercial dip such as Uncle Dan's or Good Seasons. Decorate bowl with a sprig of parsley and a radish rose or small cherry tomato.

NOTE: This can be an hors d'oeuvre tree by adding cubes of cheese, cooked ham, salami, sausage and turkey. Use it for any of your holiday entertaining.

131

Ornament Making Party

Everyone decks the halls as guests create charming ornaments for their tree. You provide inexpensive supplies, a work area and watch as guests turn artists. Refreshments can be simple Hot Chocolate and Cookies or an easy but more substantial meal of a soup, salad, bread and dessert like The Caroling Party.

MENU
Hot Buttered Rums
Hot Chocolate
Percolated Punch, page 120
Cream Cheese Logs and Crackers
Plantation Chowder, page 101
Cheese Bread, page 41
Christmas Cookies

PARTY POINTERS
- Arrange enough work space for each guest. Set up card tables for larger groups.
- Make individual "kits" of each ornament for every guest. This way you'll avoid confusion later.
- Write or type directions out on large cards or make copies for each guest.
- Have several samples of each item completed so everyone can see a finished product. You might even demonstrate the procedures.
- Guests could make cookie ornaments using the Endless Variation of Butter Cookie recipe, page 125-126. Prepare the dough ahead and arrange a table or counter area with rolling pins, flour and cutters. See Cookie Baking Party, page 121, for more ideas and details.

- Arrange to have enough scissors, small paint brushes, needle and thread and glue so that every two guests can share. One each is even better. Artists can't wait to create.
- This makes a good children's party. Keep the ornaments simple. The Tootsie Pop and Snowball would be easy enough for little hands.
- Have baskets of popcorn for stringing. Pop it several days ahead and it won't break as easily when threaded on the needle and heavy thread such as carpet thread. Have bowls of fresh popcorn for snacking.
- Guests could make **dough-art** ornaments out of this simple clay recipe:

1 cup salt
1½-1¾ cups hot water
4 cups all purpose flour

Mix salt and hot water together, stirring to soften salt. Add flour and mix well until dough forms. Knead 15 minutes. Keep in a plastic bag to avoid drying while working. Take a portion and roll out ¼" thick on a lightly floured surface. Cut out with Christmas cookie cutters. Use a straw to make hole for hanging and place on cookie sheet. Bake in 200 degree oven 1-2 hours. Ornaments should be hard to the touch and there should be no "give" when pressed. Allow to cool. Add ribbon.

NOTE: These should be sprayed or painted with a sealer.

Hot Buttered Rum Mix

This mix keeps for months in a well sealed container in the freezer.

1 pound butter
1 pound brown sugar
1 quart vanilla ice cream

In a large bowl, mix room temperature butter with brown sugar until well blended. Mix in softened ice cream until mixture is smooth. Place in a freezer container and seal well. To serve: place one tablespoon mix in a heatproof cup or mug with 1 tablespoon or more of rum, bourbon or brandy. Add 6 ounces boiling water. Top with whipped cream and garnish with nutmeg or shaved chocolate if desired.

Patchwork Ornament

This looks as if it has been quilted, yet it is quick and easy

Materials:

Styrofoam balls
Red and green fabric pieces (5-6 different patterns)
Small screwdriver or manicure orange stick
½" red velvet ribbon for bow and hanger
Straight pins
Glue

1. Cut fabric into 1½"-2" squares.
2. Place one square of fabric on styrofoam ball. Gently poke one edge into ball, continuing around remaining three sides of fabric square.
3. Place contrasting squares along one edge of previously applied piece, poking it down into the edges of second square.
4. Continue covering styrofoam ball in this manner, making adjustments for odd-shaped areas.
5. For a 3" ball, use 24" of ribbon to make a 4" loop with a smaller loop on each side. Cut ends into two points. Attach to ball with glue and secure with pins dipped into glue.

Tootsie Pop Ornament

A charming addition to the tree.

Materials for each ornament:

    1½" styrofoam balls
    1/8" wooden dowel, 4" long
    fabric in holiday colors
    18' lace, ¾" to 1" wide
    ¼" ribbon, 14" long
    embroidery thread and needle for hanger loop

Directions:

- Pat glue on tip of dowel.
- Push dowel into styrofoam ball.
- Cut fabric into a circle, 6½" in diameter.
- Sew lace to outside edge of fabric circle.
- Place fabric over ball on dowel. Secure with rubber band. Tie with ribbon just under ball.
- Sew through top of fabric and form loop for hanging on tree.

New Year's Day Bowl Buffet

Kick off the New Year with a casual party for sports fans and those who might just want to visit. Game fans gather with the T.V. in one room and others play table games, cards, or just relax and chat in another area.

No matter how you spend the day, sport fan or not, plenty of food is in order with a casual help-yourself buffet. The menu can include a variety of hot and cold finger food served throughout the game or a simple buffet of chili or soup with a fresh vegetable tray and breads. An easy dessert served with piping hot coffee is a closing to the day.

MENU
Cheese Ball, page 110
Salad
Herb French Bread
Steak Soup
Mile High Strawberry Pie

PARTY POINTERS
- Select food items that can wait well. You never know if the game will go into overtime.
- Serve Chili, page 128, with toppings
- Use Teen Age Party menu, page 164
- Or Soup Party menu, page 39-42
- Bowls of nuts and a party mix are great to nibble as T.V. crowd waits for a touchdown.

Herb French Bread

A perfect accompaniment for Steak Soup.

½ cup butter
2 tablespoons chopped chives
2 teaspoons crushed, dry rosemary
1 loaf French bread

In a small bowl mix softened butter with chives and rosemary. Cut bread in half lengthwise. Spread with herbed butter. Wrap in foil. Heat at 400 degrees for 15 minutes. Cut into 2″ slices.

Variation:

Add 2 cloves garlic, crushed to butter for a Garlic Herb Butter.

Try Cheese Bread, page 41, Parmesan Ring, page 41, Old English French Bread, page 49.

Steak Soup

A thick and hearty soup to enjoy during the game.

1½ pounds round steak, cut into cubes
½ cup margarine
1 cup flour
½ gallon (8 cups) water
1 stalk celery, diced with leaves
1 cup canned tomatoes, broken up
1 large carrot, diced
1 20-ounce package mixed vegetables
4 tablespoons beef bouillon granules or
    4 bouillon cubes
  salt and pepper taste
½ cup Burgundy wine

Brown steak in 2 tablespoons of margarine in large dutch oven. In small pan melt remaining margarine. Stir in flour until smooth. Add 2 cups water. Cook until thickened. Add celery, tomatoes, carrot, mixed vegetables, bouillon, salt and pepper to pan with steak. Stir in flour mixture and remaining water and wine. Simmer at least 3 hours. Serves 6-8.

Mile High Strawberry Pie, page 49

New Year's Eve Parties

Happy New Year! Whether you ring in the year with a big party or spend a quiet evening with friends, New Year's is a get-together time. Your neighborhood friends might enjoy not having to drive with a **Walking Progressive Dinner**; a Before the Dance gathering is a pleasant way to ease into the festivities; an **After the Dance Breakfast** is always a hit with a party crowd. For an entire evening of fun, try the **That Was The Year That Was** party where guests bring an item to symbolize an event of the past year and have guests reminiscing over the year past. Other ideas for a quieter evening might be a card or table game party; or inviting some close friends over for a potluck style meal and a chance to just visit and welcome the New Year together.

PARTY POINTERS

- A **Walking Progressive Dinner** is perfect for the neighborhood. See Progressive Dinner menus on page 149-152. Of course, the last house would serve champagne or sparkling apple juice for the non-drinking guests. Streamers, horns and hats are a festive end to the evening. Be sure to serve plenty of coffee and dessert afterwards. See Dessert Party for more ideas. Also see table decorations for Academy Awards Party, page 98-99.

- A **Before The Dance Party** is easy and serves as a pleasant transition from home to the Big Dance. If the dance does not include a meal, serve several hearty hors d'oeuvres like The Nacho Plate, page 111, and Teriyaki Chicken Wings, page 117. A Cheese Ball, page 110, Minute Pate, page 111, and the Mini Quiche, page 109, would also be good choices.

- **An After The Dance Breakfast** is a great way to continue a festive mood. Try the Omelette Party, page 26, or The Waffle Party, page 53. These are all menus that allow people to arrive at different times as they probably will. The Brunch Chapter, beginning on page 66 also has some suitable menu ideas that can all be done ahead.
- With the Omelette Party prepare all the filling ingredients and place in bowls; mix the eggs; wrap the bread in foil ready for the oven; have a dessert in the freezer or refrigerator. Put out frying pans.
- Set buffet table before going to the party so it's all ready when you return and plan a snack like Sausage Balls, page 110, for guests to nibble on as they arrive. This will give you time for last minute heating and serving.

Other Holiday Party Ideas

An Ornament Exchange, where each guest brings a wrapped ornament, homemade or purchased. Ornaments are passed in a circle and each guest selects and opens one to take home. A variation of this idea is to let the first person open his/her ornament. The next person opens his/her ornament and decides to keep it or to trade with the first person. Then the next person opens and can trade for either of the opened ones. This continues until the very last person opens a package. He or she can pick an ornament from anyone in the room.

A Christmas Luncheon takes on a special air when the tree is up and decorations grace your home. The mood is festive and joyful. Try the Luncheon, page 79. For a holiday treat serve champagne or select from any of the punches from other parties in the book.

A Christmas Brunch on a quiet Sunday slows everyone down from the hustle of the season. A nice tradition is to have a brunch the Sunday *after* Christmas each year. It's the perfect time to entertain between the excitement of Christmas and the festivities of the New Year. See Brunch chapter, page 66, for menu ideas.

A White Elephant Party is always good for some laughs. Each guest brings a wrapped, white elephant gift. Of course, the zanier the items the better. Guests exchange gifts and go home with a "new" white elephant. It also could be done like the ornament exchange where packages are opened and the next in line can choose to trade for any of the already opened gifts.

Get together with several friends and do some baking. You can double and triple batches of cookies, candies and breads so that you each have some for holiday giving. Even clean up is fun when you're talking and laughing with friends. Take a lunch break to serve soup or salad and bread and to taste some of your freshly baked products.

Wrapping gifts can be a chore but it's a delight with a friend or two as company. A few friends gather at one house with gifts, wrap, scissors, tape and tags and you all wrap together enjoying Christmas cookies and coffee.

Gourmet Groups

Gourmet Groups

A Gourmet Group is a delightful way to savor a fabulous meal without the sometimes prohibitive cost of enjoying the same kind of meal in a restaurant. Each member has a turn hosting the meal, and each member is responsible for one part of the dinner or lunch. No one is overburdened with cooking or expense and everyone has a wonderful time!

SUGGESTED MENUS FOR GOURMET GROUPS
Greek
Triopetes
Egg and Lemon Soup
Greek Salad
Mousakka
Oregano Green Beans
Greek Cookies (name)
or
Baklava

Italian
Antipasto Platter
Minestrone Soup
Tossed Salad
Italian Bread
Seafood Fettucini
Green Beans with Oregano
Zuppa Inglase

Round the World Theme

Mexican Hors d'oeuvres
Italian Soup
Roulades/German Main Dish
Greek Vegetable
French Dessert

Irish Theme

Great for St. Patrick's Day

Irish Potato Puff
Lamb Stew
Soda Bread
Trifle
Irish Coffee
Butter Cookies

French Theme

French Onion Soup
or
Vichyssoise
or
Chestnut Soup
Salad
Coquilles Saint Jacques
or
Chicken Marengo
Green Beans a la Francoise
Buttered Noodles
Croissants
or
Baguettes
A Savarire
or
Crepe Suzettes

Regional Themes
New England
Creole
Northwest

PARTY POINTERS

- **Group members** are the first consideration. Keep the size of the group to 4-5 couples. Of course you want people who enjoy each other's company because you'll be meeting regularly. Great culinary skill is not necesssary but a love of fine food and leisurely dining is a requirement.

- **A planning meeting** to discuss how you'll organize your group is efficient and helpful. Think ahead to problems that might arise, such as illness. What will you do if the hostess is ill at the last moment? Who will fill in for her or will the dinner be cancelled? What should be done if people do not arrive on time?

- Be sure to hand out **lists** with names, addresses and phone numbers of members.

- You will also want to plan **dinner dates**. How often will the group meet for dinner? Some groups meet once a month, others meet every six weeks.

- Discuss **who will bring what** course; appetizer, salad, vegetable, side-dish or dessert. The hostess prepares the main course.

- The hostess also has the privilege of deciding the **theme** of the dinner to be held at her home. She might choose an Italian, Country French or Greek theme or she might select a holiday around which to build the dinner.

- Two weeks before the dinner the hostess **calls** each member or sends invitations to remind members of the dinner, theme and dish the member is to prepare.

- Each member then **calls the hostess** a week before the party to discuss her dish. This is to assure that there will not be three courses containing mushrooms! This also alerts the hostess to any pre-planning, for example, extra room in the refrigerator for a dessert or a necessary serving piece.
- In some groups the hostess selects the **wine**, in other groups each couple selects a wine to complement the meal.
- Of course you'll not want to see the evening end, so it is fun to plan the **next dinner date** over dessert!
- Use **music** of country for background.
- Part of the fun of a gourmet group is the research and learning about cultures new to you.
- Use countries' colors for table if possible; i.e., Italy — white cloth, red and green ribbon criss-crossed on table, white napkins tied with red and green ribbon, ribbons on glasses, tiny flags tucked in centerpiece of fruits.
  Greek — Blue and white theme
  Chinese — Reds
  Italian — Red, green and white
- If you know someone from the selected country, by all means call and seek advice.
- If you're "lost" when it comes to a particular country, go your local library and ask the librarian for help. You'll find a wealth of information to help you in your planning.
- You might also try ethnic delicatessens. Owners are usually more than happy to help you learn about their own country.
- A gourmet group is a wonderful way to try unusual recipes one might otherwise never have the chance to prepare. You all enjoy a sumptuous meal with good friends without breaking the piggy bank.

Progressive Dinners

Progressive Dinner

This "traveling party" is unusual and can be lots of fun. Depending on the number of homes involved, you may find hors d'oeuvres and wine at one, soup at another, a salad at the next, the entree at yet another and dessert and coffee at the last. You could even indulge in liqueurs, another house.

The hosts need only prepare one course, so there is not the expense or the time commitment of a full dinner party, yet there is still the enjoyment of a delicious five course meal in a party atmosphere. A progressive lunch or brunch can also be fun.

MENUS
Wine and Appetizer Course
Sausage Balls, page 110
Fresh Vegetable Bouquet, page 114
Teriyaki Chicken Wings, page 112, 117
or
Mini Quiche, page 109
Nacho Plate, page 111, 112
Bacon Sticks, page 113

Soup Course
Cream of Tomato Party Soup, page 80
Vickie's Vegetable Soup, page 40
with
Cheese Bread, page 41
Parmesan Bread Ring, page 41
Herb French Bread, page 137

Salad Course

Layered Salad, page 14
Oriental Salad, page 95, 96
Favorite Tossed Salad, Choice of Dressings
served with
Crescent Rolls
or
Pita Points, page 88

Entree

Turkey Tetrazzini with Baby French Peas
or
Beef Burgundy, page 85
or
Chicken Divan
or
Chicken Supreme, page 88, with Rice and Carrots
and
Dinner Rolls

Dessert Course

Chocolate Cream Puffs, page 61
or
Trifle, page 59
or
Grasshopper Pie, page 86

After Dinner Coffee and Liqueurs

Coffee
Irish Creme, page 173
Apricot Liqueur, page 174
with
Truffles, page 18
or
Chocolate Cups with Whipped Cream, page 62

PARTY POINTERS

- Hosts and hostesses should **meet** to coordinate a meal so there is variety — not all mushroom dishes or three items with curry, for example.

- Select foods that will wait, since traveling from home to home is sometimes difficult to time.

- Allow **extra time** between homes, so guests don't feel they're on a rigid schedule. You want a relaxed atmosphere.

- Giving each guest a card with the **menu** times, homes and addresses helps avoid any confusion, and also piques interest.

- Hosts of the next course should leave the preceding home early enough to put their course out, light the candles, turn on the music, and make any other last minute preparations to welcome guests. It's easy to have such a good time at the preceding party that you are rushed to get your course ready.

- Plan foods that don't need to be cut with a knife, especially if yours is a large group and many people will have to stand.

- Some people feel more comfortable if they have a "spot" to call their own while eating. Try setting out placemats anywhere possible — coffee table, mantle, end table, desk or secretary, book shelves, piano, etc. Arrange a setting of fork, napkin and placemat in each spot. Guests don't need to sit, they just need a place to settle while they eat.

- If the group is large, 2 or 3 people could prepare each course.

- This makes a wonderful Christmas party because guests enjoy several Christmas trees and decorations. Of course, it could also have a Valentine's Day or 'Round-the-World theme.

- If the party is to be at Christmas time, you could plan an ornament or inexpensive gift exchange at the last home. Why not let someone be Santa to pass out the gifts? Ask around for a Santa suit.

- A progressive dinner can be a good moneymaker for a church or club.

MENU POINTERS

- Appetizer course: three items are enough for a group of 8-10. Add 1 more appetizer or double a recipe for every additional 4 guests.

- Soup course: for a large group select a cream type soup. Guests can drink it from a cup or mug. See Soup Party for garnishing ideas.

- Entrees: Beef Burgundy, page 85, 86, and Chicken Divan are easy to serve – all in one dish with meat and vegetable. Turkey Tetrazzini is nice with a vegetable, and Beef Stroganoff is best with rice or noodles. Decide which dish best serves your needs, and then choose a vegetable of your preference, if needed.

- Dessert course: See Dessert Party menus, page 58-64, for more ideas.

- After dinner liqueurs: See Coffee Party, page 17-19, for more ideas.

Children's Parties

Children's Parties

A birthday party to a child is a keepsake — a memory. The birthday child is king/queen for a day and his guests come to have a good time and wish him well. But a successful birthday party doesn't just happen. It takes a special kind of planning to make a party that is . . . "the best one I've ever had."

PARTY POINTERS
- Consider the age and abilities of the guests.
- Let the child have a share in the planning. Depending on age, the birthday child can help make invitations and decorations and help plan the menu and games.
- Decide on date, time, guests, theme, activities and refreshments at least 2 weeks before party.
- Send invitations a week to 10 days before party.
- Plan easy to eat refreshments.
- Write each guest's name on a paper bag so that child can have something in which to carry home favors and prizes. This saves confusion when it's time for guests to go home. The birthday child could decorate bags with stickers or felt tip pens.
- Plan more activities than you think you'll need. Nothing causes more problems at a party than a group of children with nothing to do. **Overplan** to be safe.
- A birthday party can be an important social lesson for the birthday child. Help him to greet his guests; thank each guest for the present when he opens it; see guests to door and say, "thank you for coming"; and to write short thank you notes for each gift. They're skills he'll need for life.

- Remember to have film in your camera and to take plenty of pictures for a permanent record of The Special Day. An instant camera is especially fun so even the guests can see themselves right away. For costume or face painting parties you might even want to take an instant picture of each guest and send it home as a favor.

PARTY IDEAS

- A Zoo Party (Ages 2-5)
- A Sherlock Holmes Party (Ages 6-11)
- A Come As Your Mother Party (Ages 4-11)

A special Birthday Banner can be a treasured tradition. Make a banner out of felt with a felt birthday cake and candles. Bring it out for each family member's birthday. Hang it on the front door to greet guests and announce the event or hang indoors as a decoration.

Materials for Birthday Banner

20" x 50" piece of blue felt for banner
5 1" x 2" pieces of yellow felt for flames
10" x 14" piece of white felt for cake
2" x 20" piece red felt for cake plate
1" x 8" piece of pink felt for candles
yellow, pink, blue pieces of felt for cake
    decorations if desired
1½ diameter wooden dowel, 54" long
20" x 40" piece of white or colored felt for
    "Happy Birthday" and notes
fabric glue or sewing machine

Directions:

1. Cut 2 squares, 4" x 4" out of the 20" top of large blue felt. These should start 4" from each side.

2. Fold remaining pieces in half and glue to back of banner. This forms loops for dowel hanger.

3. Cut teardrop shaped flames from yellow felt. Space evenly across center 14" of banner, one third of the way down.

153

4. Cut desired number of pink candles, 1" x 5". Glue just under "flames."

5. Cut white felt into shape of 10" x 14" layer cake, rounding top corners. Glue over candles.

6. Round edges of 2" x 10" piece of red felt for plate. Glue over cake.

7. Cut desired letters and musical notes out of white felt. Glue into place. NOTE: It's more interesting to make letters "Happy Birthday" at various heights than just in a straight line. Arrange notes at random heights.

8. Lightly sand wooden dowel and slip through top loops of banner. Hang.

Variation

- Make 3-5 felt balloons of different colors with strings made of extra thick yarn in place of birthday cake.

- Simply attach a large cluster of various colored balloons with streamers to the front door in place of a banner.

Zoo Party

A birthday party doesn't have to cost a fortune to be memorable. Here is an inexpensive party for the younger set.

MENU

Apple Juice or Orange Juice
Peanuts, Popcorn
Hot Dogs
or
Sandwiches Cut in Animal Shapes
Cake Topped with Tiny Plastic Animals
or
Cake in Cone with Animal Cracker Decoration
or
Peanut Butter Cookies in Animal Shapes

Invitations
- Cut animal shapes out of folded construction paper. Use a coloring book as a pattern. Write message inside.

- Send a balloon invitation. Blow up a balloon, but don't tie closed. Using a permanent, wide point, felt tipped marker, write all the necessary information right on the balloon. Deflate and place in an envelope with note to explain and mail to child:

> *"Blow up the balloon*
> *and you will see*
> *A message for fun*
> *to you from me!"*

155

Name Tags

Name tags can be very helpful to mothers trying to keep track of guests. It's so easy when children can be called by name. Cut tags out of same shape pattern as invitations or use purchased tags available in stationery department.

Animal Show

Guests are asked to bring favorite *stuffed* wild animal. Display them and offer prizes for each animal – the biggest, funniest, scariest, etc. Be sure there is category for each guest's animal. You could make ribbon awards and pin them with safety pins right on the animal.

Favors

Choose from tiny toy animals, sold by the bagful; boxes of animal crackers; animal shaped cookie cutters; zoo animal coloring books and a few crayons; animal cracker pins.

Animal cracker pins: Paint or spray varnish regular animal crackers, sealing both sides completely. Attach a pin-back, available in craft departments, to back of cookie with strong glue.

NOTE: Do not use this favor with children who still put things in their mouths. Be sure to tell children pins are not to eat.

Games and Activities

Be sure to have plenty of prizes. It's nice to give each participant something even if it's just a stick of gum or a small tootsie roll.

Elephant Walk: This is played like follow the leader only leader walks like different animals.

Peanut Hunt: Hide peanuts and let children hunt for them.

Trace the Peanut: Give each guest a piece of paper and a lightweight cardboard pattern of a peanut. The purpose is to trace as many peanuts as possible on a sheet of paper. This is a nice *quiet* activity.

Peanut Roll: Each player pushes a peanut across the floor with his nose. This can also be done in relay fashion.

Peanut Toss: Use a basket or ice cream tub as a target. Each player is given a certain number of peanuts to toss into the basket. This, too, can be done as a relay.

Make a Puppet: Set out small paper bags, glue, scraps of yarn, paper and scrap trim like rick rack, cording and buttons. Each child is free to create his own puppet. You could even let several guests at a time put on an impromptu puppet show for other guests.

Refreshments

Use a cake mix to make cone-cakes. Fill flat-bottomed cones ½-¾ full. Bake at 325 degrees about 20 minutes or until inserted toothpick comes out clean. Leave plain, frost or have each guest frost and decorate his own cone-cake with Cool Whip or frosting and chocolate shot or candied cake decorations. You could even provide gel cake decorators, available in baking department for guests to decorate top.

Sherlock Holmes Birthday Party

Children always seem to love a mystery and so they are sure to enjoy a Sherlock Holmes Party complete with codes, puzzles and clues.

Invitations

Children will delight in decoding their invitations. Use a code, like + = A, A = B, O = C, to write your own invitation. Be sure to include a copy of the code with the invitation.

Decorations

Make a *magnifying glass* out of poster board for the front door. Mix up the letters in "Happy Birthday" to keep the spirit of mystery. Make large *footprints* leading to the front door. Cut them out of paper or draw them with chalk on the sidewalk.

Favors

Small magnifying glasses make good favors. Or use puzzles, small books of riddles or detective story books. Play money or foil-covered chocolate gold coins would also make good favors. Use these ideas for prizes, too.

Name Tags

Make a detective's badge for each child. Write his name in code or write backwards and use as place cards. Be sure to place tape on them so the children can wear them.

Centerpiece

Place something in a box and set in the center of the table. Write a clue to what is in the box on small pieces of paper. Tape the clue to the end of a streamer going from the box to each guest's place. Guests then have a chance to guess what is in the box. The one who guesses correctly wins the prize, but provide small treats for all guests.

Games

Now You See It . . .: Arrange 10-12 items on a tray covered with a cloth. Give each guest a piece of paper and pencil and have them sit on the floor. Be sure to place the tray so everyone can see everything on it. Remove the cloth. Let everyone study the items for one minute. Then take the tray away and give children 3-4 minutes to write down as many things as they can remember. You might want to have special prizes for the guest with the most articles listed, but have something for everyone.

Musical Footprints: Use the same idea as musical chairs only make a large footprint for each guest, less one. Children must stand on a footprint instead of sitting on a chair. Remove one footprint each round.

Thumbprint Pictures: Using several stamp pads let the guests print their thumbprint on a piece of paper and use that as a starting point for a picture. Share pictures when finished.

Who Is It?: This is a simple form of charades. Give each player a card with the name of a famous character. Example: Be the wolf from "The Three Little Pigs." Or be "Spiderman." Each player has a turn acting out the characters on his card while the others try to guess.

Guess How Many Jellybeans: Fill a quart jar with jellybeans. Be sure to count them yourself. Then let guests guess the number. The one closest wins the jar. Hopefully, he'll share with guests. Otherwise he can take them home as a prize.

Other Ideas

You could play "I Spy" or have a treasure hunt.

Refreshments

Make a cake shaped like a magnifying glass. Bake two round 8"-9" cake layers and one 8"-9" square layer. Place one round layer on top of the other using a filling or frosting. Cut the square layer in half and place one layer on top of the other as with the round cake. This will form the round part of a magnifying glass and the handle. Fit pieces together to form desired shape. Frost top of round cake with white frosting and frost rectangular cake and sides of round cake with chocolate frosting. Make a rim of chocolate around edge of round cake to make it look like a magnifying glass. Write "Happy Birthday" on the white frosting and place candles on the handle. Serve with "Private Eye Scream" and "Mystery Punch" (apple juice).

Come As Your Mother Party

Little girls delight in dressing up in Mom's clothes. For this party guests and birthday girl wear some of Mom's castaway finery. Gloves and a hat are musts. Get the camera ready for this one!

MENU

Punch or Hot Chocolate
Tea Sandwiches
Small Cookies
or
Small Cream Puffs, page 161

PARTY POINTERS
- It's fun if parents can treat girls in very grown-up fashion.
- For fun ask children to bring a picture of parents and grandparents.
- Serve sandwiches on doily lined plates.

Refreshments
Punch

A quick punch is made by mixing any fruit juice with equal parts 7-Up or gingerale. Serve in plastic champagne glasses.

Tea Sandwiches

Prepare egg salad, tuna salad, even peanut butter mixed with honey and spread on bread. Cut into squares, rectangles and triangles. Or cut bread first with cookie cutters and then spread with filling. Garnish with sliced olives or a strip of pickle for a special look.

Small Cream Puffs, page 61

Small Cookies

Pass a doily lined tray of fancy cookies made by the birthday girl or purchased.

Activities

"Ladies" could play cards or games at card tables of four. Offer dainty prizes.

Decorations

Place a small arrangement of garden flowers in the center of each game table.

Favors

Give each guest a small garden flower corsage to wear. Send each "Lady" home with a small deck of cards or other treat.

Teen Parties

Teen Age Parties

Teenagers are easy to please with party fare if it's simple and bountiful. The Giant 6 Foot Sandwich and baked beans fill the bill nicely. You'll want to have some hearty snacks available as they wait for all the guests to arrive. Try the Nacho Plate and B.B.Q. Chicken Wings. And for dessert serve Double Fudge Brownies or Peanut Butter Pie. This menu will serve about 16. The Sweet Sixteen Luncheon serves 6-8.

MENU

Punch
Nacho Plate, page 111
B.B.Q. Chicken Wings, page 112
Giant 6 Foot Sandwich
Fresh Vegetables And Dip
Potato or Macaroni Salad*
Sweet and Sour Beans, page 16
Triple Fudge Brownies, page 96
or
Peanut Butter Pie, page 96

*Favorite recipe or purchased

PARTY POINTERS
- Order giant bread loaf a week ahead of time from your bakery.

- Remember you'll need a station wagon or van to pick up bread. One friend had about 1½ feet of plastic wrapped bread sticking out the side window of her compact car when she planned a party like this.
- It is handy to have a cutting board for your bread. A 6 foot long piece of 1″ x 6″ works well. Check your local lumber yard or home improvement center.
- Use 5 or 6 loaves of regular long French bread in place of 6 footer. You could even serve large French rolls and let each guest make his own sandwich.
- The Spud Party, page 43, or the Pizza Party, page 29, have great guest appeal for teenagers.
- The Sundae Party, page 50, would be a popular dessert for a teen party.
- Sometimes pre-teens and teenagers are shy and uncomfortable in social situations. That's why they especially enjoy a "Make-your-own" party. Or how about a tree cutting party, cutting trees for older citizens and then enjoying the Tail Gate Party, page 94. Or a Caroling Party, page 119, is always fun.

6 Foot Long Sandwich

Vary the filling any way you like.

1   6-foot-long loaf of French bread or 5-6
       regular loaves, sliced in half lengthwise
1   pound ham, sliced
1   pound salami, sliced
1   pound turkey, sliced
1   pound Swiss cheese
1   pound Cheddar cheese, sliced
4-6 large tomatoes, thinly sliced
3   1-pint packages alfalfa sprouts
2   large bunches leaf lettuce, washed and dried
4   large avocados, sliced
     sliced pickles, dill or sweet

"Smoosh" is a mixture of 3 parts mayonnaise to 1 part prepared mustard, with one bunch green onions, chopped if desired. Use this as a spread for both halves of the bread.

1 12-ounce jar pickle chips, sweet or dill
1 pint basket cherry tomatoes
1 15-ounce can giant olives
   toothpicks

Arrange bread on board. Spread top and bottom with "smoosh." Place a layer of lettuce across bottom. Add a layer of ham, salami, turkey, cheeses, tomato, sprouts, avocado, another layer of lettuce and sliced pickles. Put the top on loaf and cut into 4" pieces. On each piece arrange a toothpick-skewered pickle chip, cherry tomato and olive, pushing toothpick into crust. Makes about 16 servings.

Peanut Butter Pie

A peanut butter dream. It's so rich and creamy no one will guess it goes together in just minutes.

½ cup sugar
1 8-ounce package cream cheese
¾ cup peanut butter, smooth or chunky style
1 8-ounce container Cool Whip or 1 cup heavy
   cream, whipped with ¼ cup sugar
1 8"-9" graham cracker or pastry pie shell
½ cup heavy whipping cream, whipped
3 tablespoons chocolate sauce

Mix sugar, cream cheese and peanut butter until well blended. Fold in Cool Whip or sweetened whipped cream. Pour into pie shell. Garnish with dollops of whipping cream and drizzle chocolate over top. Refrigerate 2 hours. Can be frozen. Serves 6-8.

Vegetables and Dip

Cut and arrange a large tray or basket of carrots, celery, cucumber strips, broccoli, cauliflower, cherry tomatoes. Serve with favorite dip.

Sweet and Sour Beans, page 16. Double this recipe to serve 16.

Triple Fudge Brownies, page 96. Double this recipe to make about 30 servings to allow for seconds.

Sundae Party, page 50.

Use suggested amounts given to determine enough for a crowd. They'll probably consume more than you think they can.

Other Teen Party Ideas

The Pretzel Party, page 34.
The Donut Party, page 20.
The Waffle Party, page 53.

- A Graduation Party idea would be to have guests come either dressed as they will be in 10 years, or with a symbol of what they will be doing in 10 years.

- You Must Have Been a Beautiful Baby Party has guests giving host/hostess pictures of themselves as babies. Be sure pictures are carefully marked on the back. These are then displayed and guests try to guess who is who. Have a prize for the one who gets the most matchups.

Sweet Sixteen Luncheon

The birthday girl invites her friends for a delicious and rather grown-up luncheon party. Serve it in the dining room or serve buffet style and have girls sit at set card tables. Most of the time girls want to sit all together to laugh and talk — a favorite pastime.

MENU

Apricot Cooler, page 54
Oriental Salad, page 95, 96
or
Chicken Delight Salad, page 80
Pita Points, page 88
Mile High Strawberry Pie, page 49

PARTY POINTERS

- Make this a special occasion with good dishes and flatware or select from the wonderful choice of beautiful paper party goods.
- Serve Apricot Cooler in stemmed glasses tied with chosen color ribbons on glasses and napkins.
- Use birthday girl's favorite color as the theme. Tie ribbons on glasses and napkins.
- Place a small plant tied with a ribbon at each place. This is decoration plus a favor for girls to take home.

- A bowl of goldfish surrounded by shells makes an interesting centerpiece. You could even send each girl home with a goldfish in a tied plastic bag with water.
- Place a flower in the ribbon on each napkin.
- Use several flowers poked into the center of a doily and then wrapped with floral tape at each place as a favor.

That Special Touch

That Special Touch

We "eat with our eyes" as they say, so adding a garnish can make a plain Jane dish look special. There is always parsley as an old standby – a small sprig with some cherry tomatoes always adds a splash of color. Or sprinkle some chopped parsley over mashed potatoes or any dish with white sauce and it gets new life. Try some of the vegetable flowers on page 115 to add to the corners of casseroles or around platters. They are easy but impressive.

Next, you may want to try some of these easy but elegant ideas:

Frosted Grapes

An attractive addition to a ham or turkey.

1 egg white, well beaten
   small clusters of grapes
   sugar or Jello
   pastry brush

Beat egg white well. Using pastry brush, spread egg white over grapes. While wet, dip grapes into sugar or into jello. Green jello for green grapes; any red jello for red grapes. Allow to dry. Refrigerate until ready to use.

Orange and Lemon Baskets

Use for wedding showers or holidays.

Using a sharp knife, cut handle across center of orange or lemon. Cut scallops or points through center on either side of handle. Remove inside of orange carefully. Fill shell with cranberry sauce, potatoes, or vegetables and place around meat. Or fill with ice cream and freeze. Serve as holder for ice cream.

HOLIDAY GARNISHES
- Use colored eggs around Easter ham.
- Use a tiny cutter to cut heart, star, bell or even turkey shapes out of jellied cranberry sauce.

Onion Lilies

With a sharp knife, make 7-8 cuts to within ¾" of the bottom of a small onion. Place onion in ice water for at least an hour. To tint lilies, add a drop or two of food coloring to water. To make lily pad, cut a green pepper in half forming scallops. Cut piece off bottom so it will not roll. Place onion inside pepper.

Chocolate Leaves

A glamorous addition to a mousse, cake or pie.

semi-sweet chocolate
non-poisonous leaves such as holly or camellia

Line a cookie sheet with waxed paper. Wash and dry leaves carefully. Melt chocolate in double boiler over hot water or in microwave oven. Spread melted chocolate on the *back* of the leaves. Set on lined baking sheet and refrigerate until chocolate is set. Leave in refrigerator a day or two to freeze. To serve, carefully pull the leaf off the chocolate. Use leaves as a garnish for chosen dessert.

Variation:
- Use a cut out shape desired out of waxed paper or parchment paper. Use a heart, shamrock, bell, star or flower shape. Coat paper as you did leaves. Proceed as above.

Making Your Own Liqueurs

Liqueurs

Liqueurs are an elegant end to any dinner, even the simplest meal. But they can often be very expensive. Here are some easy recipes for Make-Your-Own liqueurs that require very little effort and cost a fraction of the price of commercial varieties.

PARTY POINTERS

- Any of the homemade liqueurs also make wonderful gifts either for holiday giving or as a hostess gift.

- Thrift stores are often a good source for pretty bottles for your homemade liqueurs. Ask friends to save special bottles for you, too.

Irish Creme

Jean Smith of Merlin, Oregon, shared this recipe with me. It's luscious and creamy and should be used within 3 weeks.

1 cup half and half
1 14-ounce can sweetened condensed milk
3 eggs
1 cup whiskey (Irish preferred)
1 teaspoon vanilla extract
1 tablespoon chocolate syrup or 1 tablespoon
   cocoa

Place half and half, condensed milk, eggs, whiskey, vanilla and chocolate in blender or food processor. Blend well. Refrigerate until ready to serve. Be sure to store any leftovers in refrigerator for up to 3 weeks.

Coffee Liqueur

A viewer, Becky Spintz of Portland, Oregon, wrote, "This coffee liqueur is great! I would choose it over Kahlua anytime."

½   cup instant coffee
2   cups water
1½ cups white sugar
1½ cups brown sugar
2   teaspoons vanilla extract
     one fifth vodka

In a medium size saucepan mix water and sugars. Simmer 10 minutes, stirring often. Cool slightly. Add vanilla and vodka. Pour into clear jar with lid. Store covered for 4-6 weeks.

Apricot Liqueur

This golden nectar is beautiful to serve and always a favorite with guests.

8   ounces dried apricots
2   cups brown sugar
     one fifth vodka or rum

In a large container combine apricots, sugar, and vodka or rum. Cover and allow to stand 6-8 weeks, stirring once or twice a week until sugar is dissolved. Serve as an after dinner liqueur.

The liqueur apricots are delicious in a variety of ways: Make chocolate dipped apricots. Melt semi-sweet chocolate chips in the top of a double boiler or in a microwave oven. Dip each apricot into the melted chocolate and place on waxed paper to cool. Serve as a dessert or candy.

Mint Liqueur

This liqueur is wonderful served over vanilla ice cream for a quick dessert.

1   cup sugar
⅓   cup water
1   tablespoon peppermint extract
1   teaspoon green food coloring
1-2 tablespoons glycerine
3   cups vodka (24 ounces)

Place sugar and water in a medium size saucepan and bring just to a boil. Remove from heat. Add extract, coloring, glycerine and vodka. Pour into blender or food processor and mix 10-15 seconds. Pour into clean jars; cover and allow to age 2-3 weeks.

Peach Cordial

3-4 pounds fresh peaches, peeled and quartered
2½   cups sugar
1   cup water
     Strips of lemon peel
2   cinnamon sticks, broken
5   whole cloves
1   fifth Rum
1   tablespoon glycerin

Mix sugar, water, peel and spices in saucepan. Heat to boiling, then lower heat and simmer 10 minutes until sugar is dissolved.

Place peaches in large screw-lidded jar. Pour sugar syrup over peaches including spices and peel. Add rum. Screw lid on tightly and gently shake to mix sugar and rum. Age 2-3 months. When ready to use, strain liqueur into attractive bottle. Reserve some liqueur for the peaches. Save peaches to use over ice cream or pound cake.

Other Booklets by Mary Anne Bauer

Valentine Hints: Everything to make Valentine's Day special. Gift, food, party and decorating ideas. $3.00

Christmas in July A booklet overflowing with ideas; early organizing tips, easy ways for special entertaining, recipes, gifts, simple-to-make decorations, and gifts from your kitchen. $3.00

More Christmas in July Still more ideas for getting ready for the holidays; organizing tips, entertaining with ease, quick and delicious recipes, easy-to-make gift ideas for everyone on your list – plus simple but special decorations and a basketful of gifts from your kitchen. $3.00

Hassle Free Holiday I: Entertaining and Decorating Easy recipes and simple patterns to make your holiday season a breeze.
                    $3.00

Hassle Free Holiday II: Shopping and Gift Ideas Dozens of quick and easy decorations and gifts to make, shopping tips, simple gift wrap ideas, and more. $3.00

Halloween and Fall Idea Book Everything for your Fall decoration from cornhusk dolls, fabric flowers and dough art to entertaining and recipes. An idea-packed booklet with crafts, costumes, decorations, food and party ideas. $3.00

- - - - - - - - - - - - - - - - - - ✂ - - - - - - - - - - - - - - - - - -

Booklets • P.O. Box 02467 • Portland, Oregon 97202

Please send me:
☐ Christmas in July   ☐ Hassle Free Holiday II
☐ More Christmas in July   ☐ Halloween and Fall Idea Book
☐ Hassle Free Holiday I   ☐ A Valentine Booklet

Enclosed please find $3.00 plus 60¢ postage ($3.60) for each book. If I order 3 or more books, I pay only $1.20 for postage. Total enclosed _____.

Name _____

Address _____

City _____ State _____ Zip _____
Please make checks payable to Mary Anne Bauer.

Simply Entertaining
P.O. Box 02467
Portland, Oregon 97202

Please send me_____copies of Simply Entertaining at $7.95 paperbound, $9.95 spiral bound per copy plus 75¢ postage per copy. Enclosed is my check or money order for _____.
Send to:

Name_____

Address_____

City_____ State _____ Zip _____

Please make checks payable to Mary Anne Bauer.

Simply Entertaining
P.O. Box 02467
Portland, Oregon 97202

Please send me_____copies of Simply Entertaining at $7.95 paperbound, $9.95 spiral bound per copy plus 75¢ postage per copy. Enclosed is my check or money order for _____.

Send to:

Name_____

Address_____

City_____ State _____ Zip _____

Please make checks payable to Mary Anne Bauer.

Simply Entertaining
P.O. Box 02467
Portland, Oregon 97202

Please send me_____copies of Simply Entertaining at $7.95 paperbound, $9.95 spiral bound per copy plus 75¢ postage per copy. Enclosed is my check or money order for _____.
Send to:

Name_____

Address_____

City_____ State _____ Zip _____

Please make checks payable to Mary Anne Bauer.

Index

179

180